BLACK BLOC, WHITE RIOT

BLACK BLO

AK THOMPSON

WHITE RIOT

ANTI-GLOBALIZATION AND THE GENEALOGY OF DISSENT

AK PRESS
EDINBURGH · OAKLAND · BALTIMORE

Black Bloc, White Riot: Anti-Globalization and the Genealogy of Dissent
By AK Thompson
Foreword by Bernardine Dohrn

© 2010 AK Thompson

This edition © 2010 AK Press (Edinburgh, Oakland, Baltimore)

ISBN-13: 9781849350143
Library of Congress Control Number: 2010925751

AK Press   AK Press UK
674-A 23rd Street   PO Box 12766
Oakland, CA 94612   Edinburgh EH8 9YE
USA   Scotland
www.akpress.org   www.akuk.com
akpress@akpress.org   ak@akdin.demon.co.uk

The above addresses would be delighted to provide you with the latest AK Press
distribution catalog, which features several thousand books, pamphlets, zines,
audio and video recordings, and gear, all published or distributed by AK Press.
Alternately, visit our websites to browse the catalog and find out
the latest news from the world of anarchist publishing:
www.akpress.org | www.akuk.com
revolutionbythebook.akpress.org

Printed in Canada on 100% recycled, acid-free paper with union labor.

Cover and Interior by Josh MacPhee | www.justseeeds.org

CONTENTS

FOREWORD
BY BERNARDINE DOHRN

AK Thompson's provocative meditation on the past decade of global activism, violence, race, and gender justice leaps onto the streets of our sluggish minds, upending the bricks and paving stones of the taken-for-granted, provoking the fertile young activists from whom and for whom he writes to talk back, think harder, do more. This stunning book has vibrant resonance for us too, who work to stay in the struggle—the notorious sixties generation who troubled also about whiteness, violence, and opening space to *become* while challenging Empire.

Thompson begins with the 1999 robust, inventive, horizontal demonstrations against the secretive World Trade Organization, which heralded a new era of opposition to imperialism/neo-liberal capitalism. In both content and form, the exuberant and kindred creativity on the streets of Seattle at the end of the twentieth century broke new ground—much as the New Left of the sixties transformed the paradigm of the Communist left and anti-communist fear-mongering with freedom rides, sit-ins, draft and military resistance, love/sexuality/gender liberation, and waves of cultural transformations.

Of course, 9/11 interrupted the newborn radical birthing in Seattle and troubled its baby steps, so that it was several years into the Bush/Cheney nightmare before it became apparent that a fresh conglomeration of radicalism was thriving, largely under the media radar but intermittently visible when the ruling elite gathered, and in the World Social Forums and their regional and national offspring.

Black Bloc, White Riot interrogates the early years of the anti-globalization movement for, Thompson says, "its unrealized promise"; its urgency is today all the more trenchant because of the new ripples swelling, new windows opening, struggles newly linking, altering both topography and demography.

Taking inspiration from the Zapatistas and a luminous wave of independence experiments south of the US border, ten thousand environmental justice activists gathered just this spring in Cochabamba, Bolivia, epicenter of water struggles, coca farmers, and mining, to take heed of the planet's needs for our common future. Named the World People's Conference on Climate Change and the Rights of Mother Earth, the gathering opened with a welcome from indigenous President Evo Morales to the assembled participants from 135 countries: "We can not have equilibrium in this world with the current inequality and destruction of Mother Earth. Capitalism is what is causing this problem and it needs to end." In remarkable ways across the hemisphere, the power and experiences of the previously silenced are turning up the volume: demanding greater independence from US power while seeking and finding elements of common cause with a stew of activists from the epicenter of late capitalism where the militarization of capital is experienced as totalizing.

In June 2010, some 20,000 young people filled the streets of Detroit at the second US Social Forum. The prison, health care, artist, labor, Palestinian, immigrant, housing, disabled, and justice activists and organizers present—primarily young people of color (as was the first US Social Forum)—paid homage to the elders present: Grace Lee Boggs (who turned 95 during the Forum), Vincent Harding (just turning 81), and Immanuel Wallerstein. Sixties people present were a small minority and served (generally) in solidarity and support. In contrast to the upheavals of the 1965–75 rebellions, which were largely characterized by racial and ethnic separation as a consequence of white supremacy, today's new formations tentatively and experimentally make room for what the Black Panther Party used to call "white mother-country radicals."

The zesty opening march of Forum attendees through downtown Detroit included traditional labor, noisy musical carnival revelers, feminists under the banner of Ella's Daughter (named for Ella Baker of SNCC), veterans, and anarchist formations chanting: "Not right, not left, Property is Theft!" and "Cops here, troops there, US Out of Everywhere!" Yet not one major media outlet covered the march or the US Social Forum. We did not exist. Amy Goodman of *Democracy Now* noted that twenty "tea party" activists would account for a week of blather on the news cycle but the Forum was rendered invisible, except in its own terms.

In taking as his focus an interrogation of the trajectory of white youth, the "dirty kids" who are thrown into resistance, Thompson notes Elizabeth "Betita" Martinez's germinal essay, "Where Was the Color in Seattle?" as a challenging document leading to concrete solidarity and efforts at inclusion but also to self-scrutiny. He also asserts the importance of asking why so many white youngsters of privilege got so angry, felt so alienated, and were determined to act to set themselves apart from patriarchy and the death culture through dissent, distance, and action. How do we become political people? How do we, as Grace Lee Boggs asks, learn to live differently so that others may live? And, indeed, how do we learn to live differently so we also—in the belly of the beast—may more truly, more democratically, more egalitarianly, more humanly, live?

What is it about the contradictions for white youth of the global north—more and more unbearable forms of alienation, comodification, consumption, silences, and blindness in the face of atrocity and decay, complicity in the global ecological disasters, with the long war, amid the upheavals of late capitalism—that might tear them from their relative comfort? What drives the confrontational attitude and the longing to realize the full dignity of all human beings? Thompson reminds us of the Fourth Declaration from the Lacandon Jungle, which declares that the Zapatistas are fighting for a world in which "everyone fits" and "where all steps may walk, where all may have laughter, where all may live the dawn."

I just witnessed the squats in Zurich, where young artists and activists reconnoiter, seize, and then inhabit abandoned buildings in "marginal" neighborhoods. They build artist spaces, theatres, music clubs, housing, restaurants—repairing the buildings, living communally, sharing work. They hook up to the grid, keep the police at bay and manage to work and live and create for 5–6 years until the building is re-captured by the city for private profit. Some are political organizers linked to immigrants and the marginal, some more inward. They seem practical, visionary, and determined to live toward freedom.

Black Bloc, White Riot also takes on the question of riot, of excess, of the violence embedded in tactical decentralization, away (momentarily) from social control. The book acknowledges that, tactically, some of the actions left activists isolated post-9/11, in the period of silence in the streets. It is both provocative and equivocal about violence as both the mundane template of our existence and the requisite path to political revitalization or to politics—to breaking through the suffocating society of control, what the author calls "the new enclosure."

Speaking primarily of sporadic property destruction and fleeting confrontations with police, Thompson distinguishes the riots of the anti-globalization struggles from the spectacle of terrorism. He might well agree with Simone Weil, who wrote: "Only the person who has measured the dominion of force, and knows how not to respect it, is capable of love and justice" (*The Iliad, or, The Poem of Force*).

This spring, my students and I traveled to the West Bank of Palestine, just outside of Ramallah, to observe the Israeli military courts where hundreds of youth stand criminal trial inside an Israeli military base, Ofer. There, we took measure of the dominion of force. The major charge against Palestinian youth seized by the Israeli military is *throwing stones*. This is the charge in 26.7% of military cases against children, which under Israeli Military Order 378 can result in a maximum sentence of 20 years in prison; this is rarely the sentence in but every military court case we observed, the child defendant confessed and pled guilty to avoid an extreme sentence. Evidence was not necessary. Evidence of harm was entirely lacking.

Such is the notion of youth "violence" under occupation. Such is the notion of "terrorism." Thus do youth of color at home, youth who resist around the world, and white youth who transgress become criminalized, become "threats to public safety and security." Thus is dissent regulated and policed.

Black Bloc, White Riot tackles the gender of violence, the space of politics, direct action and production, and rioting. Its author's preface ends: "I will judge this book a success if at least some consider it a useful guide in these endeavors." You will find yourself marking up the margins, disagreeing and nodding at the insights, as did I. It's important stuff. As Thompson remarks, "It is the fight of our lives."

"*I am enthroned in azure; strange as a sphinx and I;*
I blend a heart of snow with whiteness of a swan;
Abhorring changes where one line might come undone,
And I have never laughed, and I shall never cry."

—Baudelaire

"*Something very sinister happens to the people of a country when they begin to*
distrust their own reactions as deeply as they do here, and become as joyless as they
have become. It is this individual uncertainty on the part of white American men
and women, this inability to renew themselves at the fountain of their own lives,
that makes the discussion, let alone the elucidation of any conundrum—that is, any
reality—so supremely difficult."

—James Baldwin

"*It is solely by risking life that freedom is obtained; only thus is it tried and*
proved that the essential nature of self-consciousness is not bare existence, *is not*
the merely immediate form in which it at first makes its appearance, is not its mere
absorption in the expanse of life."

—GWF Hegel

PREFACE

I began this project because I didn't know what to do with myself. The year was 2002 and I'd just been laid off from my job. I applied to do a doctorate but got blacklisted. And I was broke. A friend of mine, ever resourceful, pestered me: "why don't you write a book?" It wasn't a bad idea. But there were some problems. For one, I'd never written a book before. And I didn't have a clue what I would tackle. At the time, I could barely keep my own shit together and the thought of telling other people what to think seemed daunting. Better to do it at the bar where people might forget the details than to commit it to paper. I was in distress. I ran away to the Bronx and holed up in a lover's apartment where I stayed for a month.

While I was there, a friend from back home emailed me. He was preparing his application for a prestigious academic grant and needed to pad it. "Can you remind me of the title of the collection we're co-editing on the politics of the anti-globalization movement," he asked. I responded with a list of half a dozen handles for books that could easily be judged by their cover. *Black Bloc, White Riot* was the last of them. I was about to hit send when I stopped to add one more sentence in parentheses. "(We should actually do this)," I said.

In 2002, writing a book about the anti-globalization movement seemed obvious. By the time I finished the first draft in the fall of 2004, it seemed anachronistic. I tried to persuade my friends that the movement was not actually dead—just resting, like the parrot in the Monthy Python skit. But it was useless; I couldn't even convince myself. I half-heartedly sent the manuscript to a few publishers who replied by sending me a few half-hearted rejections. Like the movement, I moved on to other things and the manuscript sat on the corner of my desk for a year.

Imagine my surprise, then, when I found a reference to the book in a communiqué released by a group of activists reflecting on the anti-G8 demonstrations in Germany in the summer of 2007. The tone of their communiqué was urgent. It suggested that a new window was opening and that we needed to be ready to squeeze our way through. Since then, that opening seems to have gotten bigger. The uprising in Greece, the student and worker mobilizations in Italy and Spain, the university occupations in New York and California, and the anticipation that now marks so many discussions about the possibility of generalized revolt against constituted power: these have all conspired to revitalize a sentiment that was effectively smothered by the painful anti-war years that stretched between 2003 and 2007.

Improbable as it seemed, I began to feel once again that there was an audience for a book such as this one. I reviewed what I'd written and realized that it might be of use to activists who never went through the ups and downs of the moment I was describing. Moreover, it seemed that there were many important lessons to be learned from this period of struggle and that these lessons weren't always effectively communicated. To be sure, my understanding of what these lessons are is different from what others believe and have written. But this is the point: from today's perspective, the anti-globalization movement is at its best when approached as an open question. The goal should not be to settle the matter by relegating the event to a bounded epochal container (as often happens when the concept of the "cycle of struggle" is mechanically applied), or by defining ourselves negatively against all the evident shortcomings of our past efforts. Instead, we should look for the unrealized promise of those demonstrations and that sensibility to determine what we can do—this time—so that they are realized.

It is this desire to realize the promise of the past that guides my reflections across the following pages. Primarily, it means looking at old events in new ways. It means considering these events as they are reflected in the mirror of an "ought" they never stood a chance of being; it means locating their promise and determining what prevented that promise from being realized; finally, it means finding the point where ruthless criticism and sympathetic understanding converge. In this respect, I've been guided in equal measure by the work of Dorothy Smith and Walter Benjamin—thinkers who find their own point of convergence in the writing of my friend, comrade, and teacher Himani Bannerji.

Like so many others, I now feel that the window is opening once again. And I would like to squeeze myself through it. But we must be careful; the gap is still narrow, and if we look closely, we can see that the window frame itself is more like a mouth of shards. By moving carefully and with deliberation, we can make it to the other side. But what will we find there? And how will we show those who follow how to get through without amassing the injuries that marred our own passage? I will judge this book a success if at least some consider it a useful guide in these endeavors.

AK Thompson
Spring 2010

F
inding a place to begin can be difficult. Let me jump quickly, then, to the hot summer of 1998 where, in Toronto, the sun made the pavement blister and desperation made the squeegee punks take off their t-shirts to show tattoos to passing traffic. It was in this cauldron of boiling tar and road rage that activists from across Canada and the US gathered for Active Resistance, an anarchist counter-convention. The event, which was raided by cops when it was held in Chicago two years prior, generated considerable hype. It is in this light that writer Jim Munroe, who spent a great deal of time capturing the political spirit of the gathering, did not limit his gaze to the scheduled workshops.

Interviewing an activist named M for a report to be published in *This Magazine*, Munroe allowed his gaze to linger conspicuously on a poignant moment. "From nowhere," he wrote, "a small punk guy with glasses comes up to M and melts into his big arms. The small punk has a gas station name-patch with BUMBOY stitched on it and M is tenderly caressing his shaved head." Like all things sublime, however, the scene doesn't last forever: "M and BUMBOY part, sharing a glance as brief as the hug was lingering..." (1998: 28).

In an article devoted to the anger and strategic vision of the new anarchist politics, M and BUMBOY's flirtatious interaction seems like a strange thing to notice. Granted, a gentle caress does make a nice counterpoint to the tabulation of extremist tendencies. And the ability to "humanize" a story has long been considered a journalistic virtue. But there's more to it than that. Munroe's story is about the activists as much as it is about the issues they seek to address. Throughout the article, invocations of dirt and disorder abound. In the first four paragraphs alone, conference participants are called "dirty kids" (not once but twice), "crusty punks," and "disease." For Munroe, there is a definite connection between this cultivated state of degeneracy and the political project at hand. "It must be admitted," he says, "the dirty kids are angry."

> Their tastes more often run to a stiff Molotov cocktail than the milk of human kindness. Injustice is everywhere. The governmental control that infuriated anarchists in the past pales in comparison with how corporations profit off of anxiety and banality and even death. It's no wonder the kids want to raze it all and start building at the grassroots. (28)

I am BUMBOY. I participated in Active Resistance and have participated in the activist and "anti-globalization" struggles that flourished and floundered over the last decade. It is not hyperbole to say that these struggles, which increased in frequency and militancy after Seattle only to fall into disarray in the years following September 11, managed (for a brief moment and in a small but significant way) to transform the world. Though the issues that activists highlighted in Seattle may not have been new, there is no doubt that resistance itself had adopted a new form (or, maybe it reconnected with something that had always been there, something lying in wait for the moment of its actualization). And though it was not on the Active Resistance schedule, Munroe captured the precursor to this "new" form in his description of the dirty kids.

■

The connection between radical politics and the people who express them is, in some ways, obvious. Since at least the time of the New Left, activists in Canada and the US have made considerable efforts to distance themselves from the loathsome mainstream. Describing the scene at Berkeley in the aftermath of the Free Speech Movement of 1964, Jerry Rubin recounted how the university—the "credential factory"—became "a fortress surrounded by our foreign culture, longhaired, dopesmoking, barefooted freeks who were using state owned property as a playground" (1970: 26). In his estimation, the university administration's fears were prompted not only by the activist's political efforts but also by their utterly foreign disposition. As Abbie Hoffman put it, when the cops confronted the hippies, they did not see peace and love and flowers. Instead, they saw "commie-drug-addict-sex-crazy-dirty-homosexual-nigger-draft-card-burner-runaway-spoiled-brats" (1969: 20).

However, if one looks just beneath the surface of these most overt skirmishes, it becomes evident that the distance between activists (or freaks, or dirty kids) and the straight world has much deeper roots. Indeed, it seems hardwired into the very concepts we use to talk about change. The etymology of the word "dissent," for instance, reveals the extent to which it is distance and distinction—rather than identity and unity—that lie at the heart of both the activist project and activism itself. On first glance, the most noticeable part of "dissent" is the prefix "dis," which implies a separation or a break. However, despite having obvious implications for radical politics, the "dis" is nevertheless not of principle importance.

Instead, things get interesting upon consideration of the suffix "sent," which comes from the French verb "*sentire*" and means "to feel." *Sentire* strongly implies embodiment. It is frequently used to describe states of wellbeing (or sickness or disease). It also has strong psychic or mental connotations, as can be judged by its appearance in words like "sentiment." Read in this way, the concept of "dissent" denotes a state of being set apart from others by a sense that something feels wrong. This separation is unsettling. It requires action, intervention. Most importantly, it suggests that dissent, although ordinarily perceived as a political category, is first and foremost an ontological one.

The word "dissident" reveals a similar connection between radicalism and modes of conduct in the physical world. Once again, the prefix "dis" implies a break. However, in the case of the "dissident," the suffix is derived from the Latin verb "*sedere*" and means "to sit." At its most basic, the dissident is the one who refuses to sit with the others. Here, political disagreement comes of necessity to take the form of a cultivated distance. In fact, without this physical and psychic separation, the dissident would be an impossible category. A complication thus arises: in order to exist as such, the dissident must set herself apart from the people but, in order for her dissent to amount to anything, she must simultaneously be with them as well.

Beyond governmental repression and corporate profiting from death, it is this ontological contradiction that defines the scope of the dirty kids' political universe; it is this contradiction that lies at the heart of radical political experience for the white middle class; and it is this social group that became most activated by the struggle against corporate globalization in Canada and the US. It is a double bind. Caught not only between the poles of capitalist social relations (where labor continues to be exploited and bosses continue their vampire

extractions of surplus value) but also between those of petit-bourgeois consciousness (where heart and mind coexist in a never-ending fratricidal feud),
the white middle class dissident incorporates schizoid dynamics into her very
being. And the question of how to be with people for whom one feels no strong
identification in the end becomes a question of how to feel anything at all.
What for Antonio Gramsci was a melancholic reflection[1] has become for the
white middle class dissident a permanent state of despair.

Why? In order to answer this question, it's necessary to move beyond
the phenomenal register in order to treat the white middle class as a socio-
historical phenomenon. Such an approach is all the more necessary given that
the middle class itself is now mostly incapable of tracing its origins and has, as
a matter of psychic necessity, for the most part forgotten them.[2]

■

In his *Reflections on Violence*, Georges Sorel argued that the emergence of a
stable middle class during the late nineteenth and early twentieth centuries
had the effect of papering over capitalism's contradictions. Since, according
to Sorel, the middle class was no longer able to connect the content of its
intellectual life to its own material interests (and often could not produce an
account of what these were), it tended to succumb to decadence and inertia. In
this way, it came to value peace—a life free of conflict—above all. This "peace"
found its precondition not in the resolution of historic contradictions but
rather in their avoidance. Neither ruthless in its pursuit of profit, as were the
bourgeois captains of industry, nor outraged by the false gravity of circumspect
policy-makers, as were the revolutionary syndicalists, Sorel's middle class was
a force of historic entropy, a decadent mass that served as ballast for a social
system caught in a storm of unsettling contradictions. And while ballast kept
the ship from being torn apart at sea, it also kept it from reaching port on the
distant shore called freedom.

Accordingly, Sorel proposed that revolutionary violence could force the
entropic mass to assume its historic responsibilities in the class war. In the
absence of violence, Sorel intoned, the decadent middle class would continue
along the course of utopian delusion.[3] Even worse, it might seduce the proletariat with ubiquitarian visions of a better world. Class war—the only means
by which the proletariat could traverse the gulf between the capitalist present
and the socialist future—could not come about "if the middle class and the
proletariat do not oppose each other implacably, with all the forces at their

disposal." Consequently, "the more ardently capitalist the middle class is, the more the proletariat is full of a warlike spirit and confident of its revolutionary strength, the more certain will be the success of the proletarian movement" (2004: 88–89).

Despite the stakes, Sorel found the middle class in France at the turn of the twentieth century ill-prepared for the challenges the class war entailed. Unlike the middle class in the United States, which seemed to still possess some of its fighting spirit, the middle class Sorel confronted seemed both enfeebled by decadence and politically neutralized by its incapacity to draw meaningful correspondences between means and ends. As far as Sorel was concerned, this situation amounted to deadly historical arrest.

> If … the middle class, led astray by the chatter of the preachers of ethics and sociology, return to an ideal of conservative mediocrity, seek to correct the abuses of economics, and wish to break with the barbarism of their predecessors, then one part of the forces which were to further the development of capitalism is employed in hindering it, an arbitrary and irrational element is introduced, and the future of the world becomes completely indeterminate. (2004: 89–90)

Unlike other thinkers working in the socialist tradition, Sorel glossed over the fact that the contradictory disposition of the middle class arose from a contradiction in the historic constitution of the middle class itself. Although the middle class is undoubtedly "one part of the forces which were to further the development of capitalism," it is shortsighted to suggest that this is its only defining feature. The "chatter" of the middle class is not a distortion of its character; it is instead constitutive of it. In the middle class, the "is" of bourgeois empiricism is forever plagued by the "ought" of bourgeois idealism. The contradiction is raw and on the surface (or else it is repressed, coiled tightly and bound by parentheses, awaiting the moment of its inevitable and catastrophic return).

Sorel's account therefore needs to be revised slightly so that we might consider how the middle class's dissident energies can be turned over to the project of radical social change. Nevertheless, by highlighting the interconnection between psychic dispositions and historical dynamics, Sorel provides an important starting point for developing an understanding of the situation in Canada and the United States today. Indeed, the pervasive myth that holds the middle class to be an existential norm (not to mention the significant

growth of a stratum concerned primarily with the economic and representational circulation—rather than production—of commodities) makes Sorel
more relevant than ever.

■

Because of the entrenchment of pseudo-managerial "work" in the Canadian
and US economy, people now encounter their productive activity with a diminishing sense of its practical outcome. To measure the distance between the
alienation of the *1844 Manuscripts* and our own depthless present, we need
only to consider the application of psychoactive drugs to the social organization of work. In their clinical reference material, GlaxoSmithKline report that
their drug Paxil can help to manage panic disorder, which they say is characterized by "recurrent unexpected panic attacks, i.e., a discrete period of intense
fear or discomfort." Possible symptoms of this discomfort include accelerated
heart rate, sweating, trembling or shaking, shortness of breath, nausea, feeling
faint, feeling that things aren't real, feeling detached from one's self, and fear
of losing control. Less acute than panic disorder, Paxil is also recommended
for the treatment of social anxiety disorder (SAD), a "persistent fear of one
or more social or performance situations in which the person is exposed to
unfamiliar people or to possible scrutiny by others."

What's so striking about these criteria is how they transform the regular
anxieties of contemporary pseudo-managerial work—where "possible scrutiny
by others" has become massive in scope—into problems that can be managed at the level of the individual. In fact, many of the problems for which
Paxil is indicated—feeling that things aren't real, feeling detached from one's
self, and fear of losing control—are nothing but the normative substratum
of late capitalism's postmodern epistemology; and though they're experienced
individually, they remain social problems throughout. The problem of Paxil's
individuation becomes explicit when GlaxoSmithKline's promotional litera-
ture is read alongside great social histories of labor like Engels' *Condition of the
Working Class in England* and Orwell's *Road to Wigan Pier*.

Remarkable for their accounts of working class tenacity in the face of in-
dustrialism, these books remain exemplary for their ability to deduce psychic
states from social organization (and vice versa); because of this, they are also
highly suggestive when it comes to considering the means by which the terms
of the social might themselves be changed. But while the transformation of
fundamental social patterns is a dream that resonates like never before, the
middle class has for the most part acquiesced to the managerial demand to

change the body/mind instead. And while GlaxoSmithKline acknowledges that "lesser degrees of performance anxiety or shyness generally do not require psychopharmacological treatment," the profit motive underlying diagnosis and prescription has led to what many experts now acknowledge to be a dangerous crisis of overmedication.

But objections based on market dynamics tell only part of the story. Psychoactive drugs are more than snake oil. They are more than means in the war against newer and more unbearable forms of alienation. Like caffeine, nicotine, and alcohol, they are part of an optimizing strategy aimed at bringing the body/mind into productive conformity with the logic of late capitalism. This logic finds its perfect object in the white middle class, a group for whom all ontological connections to the political realm have been severed.

■

Instead of politics, the contemporary middle class is constituted through government—the internalization and optimization of the capacity for productive self-control. Described famously by Foucault as pertaining to "the conduct of conduct," governmentality finds its greatest point of traction amongst the contemporary middle class. Whereas the lower classes and those resisting racial· subordination continue to know the meaning of politics and war, the white middle class's assimilation of governmentality's technologies of self-management[4] has turned it into a people that is no longer "a people" from the standpoint of conventional definitions of politics.

In this way, the indeterminate future feared by Sorel becomes forebodingly concrete in late capitalism's endless present. Harvesting deracinated fragments in the ominous shadows of the postmodern sublime, the white middle class searches in vain for a consolation prize. But a life without politics (a life without enemies) erodes the critical faculty that would allow even this minor discernment. Even in the face of a global ecological catastrophe, the white middle class remains unable to tremble before the indeterminacy of Nature, since Nature itself lost its status as ultimate Other the moment that late capitalism turned Heidegger's "house of being" into condominiums (Jameson 1991: 35). And though knowledge of the material world has not yet eroded completely, struggling with the shadows cast by its representational transposition seems for many to be the only game in town.

From Aristotle onward, being human has both entailed and mandated an engagement with politics. For Augusto Boal, politics was the highest art, the synthetic moment in which the disparate fragments of human activity get filled with consolidating meaning (1979: 11). If we accept these formulations, we must concede that their inverse must also be true: being disconnected from politics means being disconnected from one's humanity. Since this disconnection is now widely felt by the white middle class; since access to the political field (rather than its representational proxy) has been curtailed by the internalized mediations of the society of control, it's not surprising that white middle class radicalism has often taken the form (whether explicitly or not) of a struggle for redemption.

Redemption is a long way off. Deprived of genuine access to the political and supplicated by social proxies and mediations, white middle class dissidents have often been taken in by "political" gestures that are principally representational in character. Action at the level of the signified becomes impossible for those who inhabit a world in which the signifier appears to have become all. But despite the extent to which the world has endured cannibalization at the hands of its representational proxy, the contradictions underlying current forms of dissent have compelled many activists to search for what lies beneath.

In a cogent piece of auto-criticism published in the *Journal of Aesthetics and Protest*, activist Sarah Kanouse argued that the representational field with which most Canadian and US activists are familiar by virtue of their class location can't be taken to be all of (or the most important piece of) the political sphere. Reflecting on the popularity of culture jamming and similar practices, Kanouse pointed out how "the attention of prankster activism to the superstructure, to use an old fashioned term, underscores the upper-middle-classness of its politics."

> The arena of consumption, the terrain engaged by pranksters, is where most middle-class people develop their identities, form their allegiances and live their politics. It's a key site for engagement, and pranks can be seen as contemporary popular education for those who already have a voice in consumer society... What gets lost in the shuffle is the fact that radical social change is not merely the adoption of a different set of consumer habits and the reality that attaining global economic and environmental justice will entail a high degree of sacrifice for those of us in the world's top income brackets. (2005: 28)

Despite covering familiar terrain, Kanouse's comments nevertheless manage to cut to the heart of the matter. How else are we to understand the fact that her critique of representational action leads directly into a discussion of "sacrifice"—a religious, ontological, and (genuinely) political category of the first order? Hidden in the grammatically passive voice and conditional tense of her account of "attaining global economic and environmental justice" lies the recognition that—whether it's elected or imposed—the advent of a post-representational political moment will be heralded by violence.

Today's dissidents exist in an indeterminate space between signified and signifier, between politics and its representational proxies. It's an untenable position marked by psychic instability. It is therefore not surprising to find that white middle class activists tend over time to be reabsorbed into the representational sphere or (on rare occasions) to be seduced by the violence of genuine political—and, hence, human—being. Here, the point where the infinitude of abstract possibility is supplanted by the unforgiving specificity of the thing selected, the dissident enters the realm of genuine politics. It is a moment of clarity available only to those who can make concrete what had previously been unthinkable. Guarding the door between the thinkable and the unthinkable, between the political and its proxy, stands violence.

If this is true, then the anxious subterranean meaning of the claim that the anti-globalization movement was a coalition formed around "one no and many yeses" becomes instantly clear. Ordinarily, activists read this slogan as suggesting that our rejection of capitalist globalization (that thing that binds us together) does not in and of itself curtail possible visions of freedom (the many yeses to which we aspire). However, in light of our current discussion, we must at least contemplate the possibility that our "one no" applies not to the rejection of capitalist globalization but rather to our nearly univocal refusal of the moment of decision demanded by politics. Correspondingly, the slogan's "many yeses" are our proxies, our prankster politics, the myriad ways we distract ourselves while deferring the inevitable.

■

On first blush, the claim that the anti-globalization movement in Canada and the US was white and middle class appears susceptible to both easy agreement (in which case the claim itself becomes banal) *and* to easy refutation (since it is equally evident that resistance to globalization was more than just a white thing). But whatever the ultimate truth of these superficial observations, many activists and social commentators were quick to highlight the whiteness of the movement and, on occasion, its middle class character too. In response, other commentators endeavored to highlight the movement's putative diversity. Still others aimed to shield the white middle class from critique by recasting it as a legitimate claimant to the mantle of resistance.

This last process can be seen in the work of movement participant and theorist-chronicler Amory Starr. In the Introduction to her *Global Revolt*, Starr lists and then responds to thirteen "myths" about globalization and the resistance against it. Last in·this list of myths is the claim that the "opponents of globalization are romantic Luddites, alienated punk rock kids hopping from summit to summit on 'protest tours.'" In response, Starr argues that "these distorted images trivialize the suffering and rage of the working classes and youth of the North, where resistance movements are still marginal, but growing." However, in conclusion (and as a seeming *non sequitur* to all that came before), she reminds us that "the Global south is the real point of impact" (2005: 9).

At least two distinct maneuvers are at work here. First, those protesting in the global north are depicted as belonging to a class of people whose revolt is both legitimate and intelligible (or, at least more so than if they were middle class, as critics had suggested). However, since the only evidence that Starr provides for her characterization of the movement's class composition is its "suffering and rage," it's hard to imagine the concrete basis upon which she sets those she champions apart from the "alienated punk rock kids" of the myth she sets out to debunk.

Next, movement resistance is further legitimated by being spot welded to the struggles of the global south (where the real action is said to be taking place). But here too, a logical problem thus ensues: either the movement was really taking place in the global south (in which case the activists championed by Starr get more attention than they deserve) or it was not (in which case she must contemplate how alienated punk rock kids might be conceived as viable political claim-makers). To be sure, the opposition to neo-liberal globalization was more than one thing. And the protests in Seattle were by no means the first expression of resistance to the reorganization of the planet. Nevertheless, what developed on the streets of Seattle amounted to a "structure of feeling"— to use Raymond Williams's apt phrase (1977: 128–135)—that forged a link between movement activity and the anxieties and aspirations of the white middle class. In Canada and the United States, this white middle class gave shape to the movement. To it, we can attribute both the movement's successes and its ultimate failure.

To be clear, the racial and spatial delimitation of my investigation should not be taken to suggest that other figures and forces were not active participants in the fight against neo-liberalism's new global enclosures. Indeed, many people legitimately trace the origins of such movements to the Zapatista uprising in the Lacandon Jungle. Similarly, although they did not orient themselves to the anti-globalization movement itself, many working class and people of color-led social movements active in Canada and the US around the time of Seattle struggled against aspects of the neo-liberal project. The movement for prison abolition and the Justice for Janitors campaign are but two obvious examples of struggles that addressed neo-liberal issues while operating outside of the anti-globalization milieu.

The differences between these forces and the anti-globalization movement are not merely idiosyncratic. Movements are shaped by their participants. Because of this, the anti-globalization movement became a vector for the expression of white middle class sensibilities and conceptions of struggle. For many radicals who remained on the movement's periphery, these sensibilities oscillated between annoying and incomprehensible. My goal here is to make these peculiar features intelligible in order to determine whether there's anything to be salvaged. It's important to note, however, that this isn't exotic anthropology. Although the movement was particular and peculiar, many of its sensibilities were drawn from sources that enjoyed broader resonance. These sensibilities were easily transposed into the register of the movement's white and middle class relevancies; in fact, they often seemed to speak directly to a pervasive form of turn-of-the-century middle class anomie.

For instance, Peoples' Global Action made clear in their Hallmarks that, alongside their rejection of capitalism, their emphasis on tactical decentralization, and their commitment to a confrontational attitude, they strove to "embrace the full dignity of all human beings." Although the general tenor of the PGA Hallmarks instructs us to read this proclamation with the oppressed in mind, the open-endedness of both its "full" and its "all" left room for white middle class radicals to consider how their own experience was an unbearable symptom of a world gone mad. Similarly, in their Fourth Declaration from the Lacandon Jungle, the Zapatistas made clear that they were fighting for a world in which "everyone fits" and "where all steps may walk, where all may have laughter, were all may live the dawn." For white middle class activists (who found themselves reflected in everything but held by nothing), the promise of a world in which everyone fits could not help but compel an interrogation of the price exacted by privilege.

As the movement developed, activist critiques of progress and privilege began to draw inspiration from the cultural patterns of indigenous peoples.

Although the details of these "traditions" were often mythologized beyond recognition, they nevertheless enabled white middle class radicals to locate an extrinsic referent that could help to guide them beyond the horizon of neo-liberalism. This process has been rightly condemned for its habit of appropriating and rendering exotic the quotidian stuff of other people's lives; however, it's important to note (as Hal Foster did in a different but parallel context) how "partial identification with the primitive, however imagined problematically as dark, feminine, and perverse, remained a partial disassociation from white, patriarchal, bourgeois society, and this disassociation should not be dismissed as insignificant" (2004: 8).

Commenting on the extensive interest in indigenous ways of life that she noted within the movement, Starr reports how these "advanced traditions, developed in societies in which the market (to the extent it existed) was subordinated to social criteria, are now posed as 'alternatives' by movements which dare to redefine progress as something other than surrendering history, culture and life to business."

> Survivors of postmodern capitalism are embracing these traditions as methods of achieving their most sophisticated aspirations for sustainable, accountable, diverse and engaged social life. (2004: 51)

Although they are not the stated subjects of her investigation, Starr's account reveals the extent to which the movement's structure of feeling was shaped by white middle class preoccupations. For these "survivors of postmodern capitalism," identification with a mythically valorized "outside" at odds with their own experience helped to give shape to their struggle. It gave it its reference points and its themes. In this way, the movement's structure of feeling came to express symptomatic preoccupations that were not restricted to legitimate concern for the plight of those in the global south. Camille de Toledo recounts how, for those in the global north who came of age during neo-liberalism's ascent, "the new spirit of revolt isn't economic. It's respiratory ... a claustrophobic reaction to the idea that the world is a finished piece of work" (2008: 9). The goal of *Black Bloc, White Riot* is to take this respiratory distress seriously.

■

Ten years have elapsed since Seattle. During this time, N30 has come to mark a new way of thinking about politics, globalization, and resistance. And though it has begun to lose its luster, it's a dream that won't die. The decline of the movement's first phase in Canada and the United States allows us to measure how much we won and lost. But while much has been written on the subject of neo-liberalism and the injustices it inspires, and while there has been no shortage of ink devoted to the movement as an organizational novelty, relatively little attention has been paid to the new dissidents themselves. Those accounts that do exist have tended to view the movement's overwhelmingly white composition as a problem to be solved rather than as a thing to be explained. This tendency first emerged with (and still owes much to) the publication of Elizabeth Martinez's "Where Was the Color in Seattle?"

Cited as a matter of course whenever activists are in the mood for self-criticism, Martinez's article provided a functional template upon which writers could build when evaluating subsequent actions. So extensive was the piece's influence that it even became the basis for organizing efforts. San Francisco-based Anti-Racism for Global Justice (ARGJ) formed in 2000 with the specific intention of operationalizing Martinez's insights. In their promotional material, the group describes how—as members of a younger generation of white anti-racist organizers—they "came out of the movements for global justice that rocked the WTO in Seattle and are [now] actively involved in the growing anti-war movement." Their debt to Martinez is explicit: "We were inspired by Elizabeth 'Betita' Martinez's highly influential essay 'Where was the Color in Seattle?' which highlighted the need for white activists to examine racism and how it affects our organizing."[5]

Self-criticism is an important skill, especially when the critics have the wherewithal to operationalize the critique. However, while the profusion of articles and organizing efforts owing a debt to Martinez have all highlighted the extent to which American anti-globalization protests were often overwhelmingly white affairs, they have not tended to engage this fact from the standpoint of whiteness itself. And while self-reflection has yielded important insights, little attention has been given to the fact that the explicative category itself needs explaining. Consequently, indictments of the movement premised on its whiteness have often left activists with little more than a self-evident (and occasionally moralistic) injunction to make organizing efforts more inclusive.

This is not to say that inclusion is unimportant. However, since it focuses almost entirely on a "solution," the rush to inclusion has often overshadowed the need to look at the specificity of the problem itself. There is no doubt that the movement in Canada and the US was disproportionately white. And many radicals agree that this representational distortion made it more difficult for people of color to engage. What remains to be addressed is why it was that so many white kids got caught up in the struggle in the first place.

How is it that a militant movement seemed to emerge spontaneously from white middle class spaces like the campus and the suburb—spaces where "oppression" can often seem like an abstract category? How did the "dirty kids" get angry—and why did they feel so ill at ease in their world of plenty despite the undeniable privilege their circumstance afforded? Why did they seem to become their politics and pronounce them as ontological truths? Why, finally, did they seek to mark themselves apart from the world from which they came— as though, through distance (both conceptual and physical), they might purify themselves once and for all? Important in their own right, these questions also help us to plot the points of a constellation that connects these recent experiences of struggle to a longstanding tradition of dissident ambivalence.

It's difficult, for instance, to overlook the remarkable similarities between the anti-globalization movement's structure of feeling and the one that pervaded New Left struggles. One compelling way to understand this historical relay is to highlight the unresolved contradictions underlying the experience of the political dissident. Practically speaking, this means paying attention to the manner in which both New Left struggles and our own more recent upheavals placed special emphasis on the question of *becoming*. More generally, it means following the thread running through the heart of struggle and training our ear on its reverberations.

John Sanbonmatsu has concerned himself with precisely these reverberations. In *The Postmodern Prince*, Sanbonmatsu points out how the New Left shared in the Protestant Reformation's structure of feeling. "To those caught up in it," he explains, "the movement, which provided a new existential and spiritual model of self and other, seemed at times to prefigure a New Jerusalem" (2004: 31). Similarly, in *The Voice and the Eye*, Alain Touraine suggests that the new social movement call for "self-management" during the 1960s acted "as a conveyor of the dream of community independence." In this way, it revived "the peasant dream of a generalized middle class which would be both productive and managerial" (1978: 22).

From our present vantage, it's easy to see how important aspects of the New Left's structure of feeling—identified by both Sanbonmatsu and Touraine as drawing upon (mythical versions of) the utopian anti-capitalist peasant consciousness of the seventeenth and eighteenth centuries—also found expression in the anti-globalization movement in Canada and the US. The celebrations of productive-managerial autonomy and the dreams of "community independence" marking those years are hard to ignore. Because of this, I propose to reorient the terms of investigation so that—rather than focusing on "inclusion" as a self-evident good—we make white middle class socio-psychic indeterminacy the motive force in a genealogy of dissent. This indeterminacy can be located in time and space and considered in relation to the social contradictions that produce it. In contrast, the activist rush to inclusion has often made it difficult to consider the specificity of the white middle class as a social problem.

Although it betrays activist commonsense, I propose that it's worthwhile to investigate the anti-globalization movement that emerged in Canada and the US *as* a white middle class phenomenon. Although the movement was self-evidently more than one thing, its role as a laboratory in which white middle class activists sought to exorcize their constitutive contradictions and regain the capacity for political being should not be overlooked. It's just as important, however, to avoid reading this struggle in the laboratory solely in accordance with the conventions of the personal redemption story. Middle class anguish has historically found resolution just as regularly in the mytho-poetics of the far right as it has in the process of genuine liberation. And so, while I can empathize with readers who feel no personal interest in poor little rich girl stories (for readers who cringe at the thought of another book about white people), the political stakes of the drama cannot be responsibly ignored.

In advancing this proposition, I am not arguing that the movement was entirely white or, for that matter, entirely middle class. I am certainly not arguing that people of color should not get involved and participate as they see fit, or that white activists should not try to make our organizing efforts more relevant and open. What I am saying, however, is that there is a danger of mistaking specificity for exclusion. By not looking at the specificity of the movement (by not grappling with the interesting and sometimes difficult contradictions that arise when people with considerable social privilege adopt radical postures), we lose sight of the material shape of our struggle. Anti-racist theorists have for a long time noted that whiteness tends to get expressed as an abstract universal; as a standpoint that isn't a standpoint; as something that goes without saying. And while activists have made considerable strides in our attempts to denaturalize whiteness, the race to inclusion often ends by occluding the specificities of whiteness in favor of what are perceived to be the greater, more grounded, and real specificities of the included other.

If the white middle class is going to struggle (and it has its own reasons for doing so quite apart from playing the role of ally to the most oppressed), it is necessary that it begin to do so on the basis of a concrete understanding of its own conditions of possibility. And so, while the exemplary resistance of militants in the global south inspires me, and while the courage of those fighting occupation in North America's internal colonies demands huge respect, this book is not about them. To be sure, it's important that these struggles are not sidelined or forgotten. Just as important, though, is reckoning with the specific character of white middle class dissent. Concretized in moralistic slogans (reminding us that resistance "didn't start in Seattle"), the movement's rush to inclusion uncovered one truth only to bury another.

■

Whiteness is a specific experience. It arises from specific social locations and allows for the cultivation of specific capacities. One manner in which these specificities have been expressed historically is through the perceived connection between whiteness and death. For Richard Dyer, this connection is made possible by (and finds its first expression in) the Christian notion of spirit—that thing which is in but not of the body. By imposing a constitutive tension in being, the spiritual conceits of white ontology produce tremendous capacities for self-realization. They also produce a systemic anxiety that cannot be resolved within the terms available to whiteness itself. For Dyer, the counterpoint to white people's self-aggrandizing spiritual transcendence is the fear that they are not here at all. Is it any wonder, then, that Paxil has found such a devoted following by promising to deal with the feeling that things aren't real?

The productive schizophrenia of the white middle class (the pathological state in which people strive to simultaneously be *of* and *more than* this world while never reckoning with its concrete and unforgiving specificity) finds perverse expression in the pantheon of undead creatures that populate horror films. Consequently, these films may be treated as therapeutic exercises, staged reenactments, or even as so many returns to the site of trauma. For analysts of whiteness, they offer an unexpected opportunity to read through the manifest content of everyday life in order to uncover the latent traces of something that can't be expressed directly. According to Dyer, zombie movies exploit the simultaneity of white people's fear of and fascination with death. Describing the final act of George Romero's *Night of the Living Dead*, Dyer recounts "an aerial shot of some white figures moving across a field in a shaggy line, with slow, terrible deliberation."

We assume they are zombies, since this is always how they have been shown in the film; yet, when the film cuts to a ground level shot of these figures, we realize that they are the vigilantes (all of whom are white) come to destroy the zombies. There is no difference between whites, living or dead; all whites bring death and, by implication, all whites are dead (in terms of human feeling). (1997: 211)

This thesis becomes all the more compelling when one considers how, in *Night of the Living Dead*, the death impulse that overtakes the white characters finds its counterpoint in the figure of Ben, the resourceful Black man who keeps his shit together while his allies lose it by going catatonic or succumbing to the urge to devour one another. Citing liberally from the visual history of lynching, the last scene of the film sees Ben shot dead by the vigilantes. According to Dyer, *Night of the Living Dead* yields both horror and catharsis for white viewers who must confront their own ambivalent proximity to death. The political implications of Dyer's analysis become explicit when one remembers the tremendous debt Romero's film owes to the political climate— Black Power and civil rights—of the period in which it was made.

Lest this foray into the overgrown (and over-fertilized) fields of psychoanalysis and cultural studies be dismissed as fanciful or idiosyncratic, it's useful to remember the many antecedents to Dyer's analysis. Among these antecedents, one of the most striking ("striking" because of its unresolved and contradictory character) is to be found in the work of Antonin Artaud. In 1938, Artaud suggested that Europe's lack of culture could be explained on account of its inability to connect with magic. Experienced for the most part as a gnawing but undecipherable anxiety, the problem of white lack becomes explicit at the point of the colonial encounter. White death marks the moment. "If we think Negroes smell bad," begins Artaud, "we are ignorant of the fact that anywhere but in Europe it is we whites who 'smell bad.'"

> And I would even say that we give off an odor as white as the gathering of pus in an infected wound. As iron can be heated until it turns white, so it can be said that everything excessive is white; for Asiatics white has become the mark of extreme decomposition. (1958: 9)

Although Artaud's account (like Joseph Conrad's "horror" story before it) transposes concrete historical details into the more malleable register of metaphor, the persistence of the fascination he taps into cannot be ignored.

Like a neurotic repetition compulsion, the white anxiety with death finds its contemporary expression in the nervous injunctions regularly issued by the army of white middle class dissidents striving to *really* live. And, since the historical contradictions from which it arose have yet to be resolved, it's hardly surprising to find that the themes, modes, aesthetics, and anesthetics of the movement in Canada and the US all reflected this anxiety.

Because it arises from a specific ontological incongruity, the white experience of constitutive lack is far from universal. It is thus a grave problem that white activists sometimes talked about anti-globalization struggles as though they were *the* movement, *the* inevitable and correct response to neo-liberal barbarity. This problem found its counterpart in the inverse proposition occasionally advanced by radicals who asserted that—because the movement was primarily a white phenomenon—it was either unimportant or dangerous from the standpoint of revolutionary social transformation.

In opposition to both of these positions, it's necessary to advance the more modest (but also more politically demanding) proposition that the movement was *a* response—one that allowed white activists to begin confronting their expulsion from the political field while engaging in concrete solidarity with activists struggling around other issues, under different conditions, and by other means. In order to actualize the promise of this moment, it is necessary to deal with the specificity of white experience and reckon honestly with the knowledge it yields. It is the minimum precondition to having more than good will to bring to the coalition table.

■

If it was not already clear beforehand, the decade since Seattle has made clear that the knowledge arising from white dissident experience is as contradictory as white dissent. Almost from the outset, the anti-globalization movement in Canada and the US was gripped by a series of confusing tensions. At first, these tensions were expressed abstractly through antithetical pairs like "violence" and "non-violence," "summit hopping" and "local organizing," and "direct" and "mass" action. Although the discussions were not always clear, there was no shortage of debate about either these terms or their implications. For the most part, however, the issues were left unresolved. But rather than weigh in on these debates as they were originally conceived, my objective is to consider how the *framing* of these debates can tell us a great deal about the activists that engaged in them.

Each chapter in *Black Bloc, White Riot* deals with one of the debates arising from these abstract antithetical pairs. By considering how activists sought to make sense of the world, and by following debates as they unfolded over time, I aim to make visible the contradictions underlying the dissident experience of white radicals. Since I'm one of those radicals, this project has been both illuminating and unsettling. However, it's not my intention to leave this work at the level of diagnosis. After all, we hardly need a book to tell us we're fucked up. Nor would I find it satisfying to restrict my efforts to phenomenological description, as if—by revisiting the site of trauma—white activists might exorcise the spectres of embodiment and specificity once and for all.

What does seem worthwhile is tracing the concrete means by which engagement in struggle changes people by bringing them closer to the decision that inaugurates political being. Despite our ultimate failure, many of the activists that participated in the movement are demonstrably different for having engaged in conflict. And activists (who have often pointed out how struggle brings them to a clearer sense of themselves) seem to know this intuitively. In the closing six panels of his squatting opus *War in the Neighborhood*, New York-based comix artist Seth Tobocman makes the connection between struggle and ontological transformation explicit:

> If we can look at an abandoned building and imagine it full of people if we can look at a vacant lot and imagine a garden, / then why can't we look at each other and imagine what we can become with time and work? / It is a good thing to take up the struggle against oppression / it is also a good thing to make mistakes in that struggle and grow wise. / How else would we come to know ourselves? (1999: 328)

Recognizing activism's tendency to transform people is not new. However, what remains to be determined is *how* this transformation occurs. In each of the following chapters, I contend that it was the excessive character of the movement—its riotous exuberance—that enabled activists to reach beyond the ontological constraints of the white middle class. As practical experiments with violence, these moments of excess provided functional (if incomplete) conduits into the realm of political being. In turn, this new and unknown universe provided activists with a novel point from which to consider and participate in movement debates. And while violent exuberance did not always lead to clear answers (and while it may not have always appeared to be tactically efficacious), it nevertheless enabled us to ask the old abstract questions in new concrete ways. By passing through violence, activists began to move away from the representational coordinates of the society of control and toward the uncharted territory of a post-representational politics.

Despite its profound tactical limitations and incomplete realization, the movement's experiments with riotous excess threw us before decision. It deposited us at a fork in the road and asked us to consider whether we were ready to cease being critics of society and start being conscious producers of it instead. Were we ready to become political? For a brief moment, the excess of our riot seemed to demand a decision we could never take back.

■

We betrayed our moment. The silence in the streets over the last few years bitterly confirmed that turning back remained more than possible for most of us. Most anti-globalization-era activists did not follow the trajectory upon which they had begun plotting their course to its logical conclusion. Like the canary in the coalmine and the sacrificial lamb, those that sought to complete their actions found that they had ventured where the movement as a whole dared not tread. Cut off from mass mobilizations and acting in isolation, these figures quickly became targets for state agencies.[6] It's easy to condemn them; from the standpoint of tactics, their actions seem both ill advised and adventurist. Nevertheless, it remains necessary to acknowledge the basic truth of their actions when considered from the standpoint of politics. It's a truth made manifest in the language of an ontological transposition. It is a decision that will be hard to undo.

In calling this book *Black Bloc, White Riot*, I hope to highlight the remarkable similarity between the ontological conflicts of the white middle class and those analyzed by Frantz Fanon in *Black Skin, White Masks*. As with Fanon, who found the "black man" to be a logical impossibility, I am interested in documenting the precise means by which the category "white middle class political being" is experienced in the first instance as a contradiction in terms. Although beginning from opposite ends of a world cut in two, *Black Bloc, White Riot* and *Black Skin, White Masks* both argue that ontological impossibilities can only be resolved by changing the world (that they are not representational problems but practical ones). And "changing the world" is a task that can only be carried out by political actors. These actors do not magically appear. They must demonstrate the truth of their being through decisive action. They do so by passing through violence.

A second (and perhaps more obvious) inspiration for *Black Bloc, White Riot* is "white riot"—The Clash manifesto penned in the age of No Future. In it, Joe Strummer addresses the envy and frustration he felt upon witnessing violent Black responses to police repression during the 1976 Notting Hill carnival. Although British whites of the same period were confronting diminishing standards of living with the onset of neo-liberalism, Strummer felt that the twin evils of school and fear of jail—the ideological and repressive state apparatuses considered by Althusser—kept them from producing an adequate response. Seduced by their nominal inclusion in the society of control, whites were unable to assume the responsibilities of political being as Blacks had. In Strummer's lyrical universe, there were only two choices: "are you taking over / or are you taking orders?" Violence either writes a new law or preserves the one that exists. For those that feel the weight of the unbearable present, there is only one acceptable decision.

As for the Black Bloc of my title, I must concede that some of my readers will be disappointed. This is not a confession or a memoir. Indeed, I've tried to keep the salacious gossip to a minimum. Although the Black Bloc has a history, although it can be investigated journalistically, and although it has all the attributes of a concrete sociological phenomenon, I have chosen to approach it in a different fashion. In what follows, the Black Bloc is considered primarily in its role as limit situation for the white middle class. I argue that it marks the point at which some of us began to pass through violence and show signs of a new kind of political being. To be sure, this transformation was personal. Nevertheless, it had practical pedagogical implications for anyone that cared to take note. And while it's difficult to get a clear sense of the extent to which this transposition took hold, hints can be gleaned from the fact that the questions that plagued the movement in earlier periods could later be posed in new, different, and often better ways.

■

What follows is a particular account. Though they all stand in relation to the movement, I do not pretend that the events discussed in these pages represent—or could represent—the whole picture. Indeed, while some of the demonstrations, events, zines, and websites I consider will be familiar to most activists, some will undoubtedly seem curious and esoteric. However, since my goal is to look at each instance with an eye to what lies beneath (since what is at stake are the procedures that go into the making of a moment), readers are encouraged to trace out implications for other settings. *Black Bloc, White Riot* is less a general overview of the movement than it is a way of demystifying movement events.

Central to this approach is a concern with how class location simultaneously shapes experience while, at the same time, making the conditions that enable that experience difficult to perceive. Rather than presupposing an extrinsic point from which these dynamics might be observed objectively, I've chosen instead to trace their expression in forms of everyday talk and action. "The discursive" and "the material" are thus considered in their full interpenetration. And so, while forms of talk are not *caused* by the economic in any simple sense, they nevertheless give expression to its features and, as such, provide a ground upon which to conduct analysis.[7] How does the manner in which these debates were first conceived express the enabling and constraining features of the social base from which they arose? More importantly, how are we to make sense of the fact that, through the course of struggle, the manner in which these debates were conceived and carried out began to undergo a dramatic transformation?

As I will argue throughout this book, central to this transformation was the fact that—at certain threshold moments—movement politics began to lean away from the field of representation and toward that of production. In each of the following chapters, I highlight some of the moments in which this transformation began to take place in order to consider the means by which it became possible.

Starting from the standpoint of ontology, my concern is primarily with the means by which the political field itself is constituted. And though my central claim—that the movement from representational distortion to politics proper passes through violence—seems to have been intuitively grasped more easily by the anarchist wing of the movement than by its social democratic counterpart, there is nothing within anarchism itself that prevents it from getting ensnared in the representational domain. After all, even DIY ethics must come to terms with the fact that—at present—it primarily represents people's *intention* to become direct producers. In truth, most of what actually gets "produced" remains representational in character. Zines, records, and bicycle tube bondage gear are all fun. But given the enormity of the world and of our responsibility to one another, we should not become seduced by the idea that these representational endeavors correspond in any sense with the demands of the political.

With this in mind, the organization of the following chapters roughly follows the arc along which the movement traveled as it passed from a state shaped primarily by representational "politics" toward one marked by political decision and proximity to violence. In order to understand this progression (and because the term tends to elicit strong reactions), it's necessary to clarify what is intended here by "violence." Keeping with the ontological thrust of my argument, the conception of violence upon which this work is based presumes two fundamental and correlative attributes. First, violence is the name of the general principle by which objects are transformed through their relationship to other objects. Second (and as a result of the first), violence is both the precondition to politics and the premise upon which it rests.

Why? In the representational field, "identity" is the name given to the absolute correspondence between an object and the concept by which it is denoted. In contrast, violence is the name of the process by which objects are transformed so that they no longer correspond to the concepts to which they had previously been tied (as when "architecture" is magically rematerialized as "property" the minute you set it on fire). Or, in another variation, violence marks the moment when an object maintains its conceptual integrity—its self-sameness, its identity—at the expense of another object seeking to do the same. By reducing violence to its basic ontological premise, it becomes clear that neither being nor becoming is possible without it. The pressing question, therefore, is not whether or not to engage in violence. Instead, it is to decide what we ought to become.

An inevitable danger associated with reducing violence to its basic onto-logical premise is that, by creating a conceptual space in which anything (from breastfeeding to writing an email) can be considered "violent," the term itself can appear to lose all meaning. But rather than exempting these apparently benign forms, it's more honest to recognize the violence implicit in mundane and everyday acts. For instance, the meaning of a mother's declarations of sub-jective autonomy is radically unsettled at the very moment her child takes her for food. The conceptual link between the mother and the idea of autonomy is severed; she must struggle to reconstitute it on new grounds. However, pre-cisely because such violence is ordinary (precisely because it corresponds to an ascribed logic of production wholly commensurate with the established order), it is rarely recognized as such.[8]

It thus becomes clear that—as a political question—violence is always sub-ject to a threshold of recognizability. The violence of the movement (which, for the most part, was limited to sporadic property destruction and fleeting confrontations with police) was much closer to this threshold that is the nurs-ing mother considered above. This movement toward recognizability arose in part from the tremendous energy that activists committed to their efforts; however, the significance of the threshold arises not from the intensity of the effort but from the fact that the effort itself implied a production at odds with constituted power.

In other words, the threshold of recognizability corresponds to the point at which the productive dimension of violence begins to cross over into politics. These dynamics are normally perceived as though through a *camera obscura* where, if it's not "political," it's not recognized as violence. From the millions of animals that meet their end in factory farms to the persistence of the nuclear family and its need to traumatize children in order for them to turn out "well adjusted," the presumption that politics precedes (and, hence, mitigates) violence has become a central tenet of the society of control. Nevertheless, a closer investigation reveals the extent to which the sequential order of the terms under consideration is exactly the opposite of what it at first appears to be. Furthermore, the fact that oppositional violence comes into view as a result of its proximity to the threshold of recognizability should not cause us to lose sight of the fact that both order and challenges to order abide by the same productive—which is to say violent—premise.

Considered in this way, it becomes clear that violence shares many attibutes with the conception of labor elaborated by Marx in Chapter VII of *Capital*. However, unlike labor, which requires that the producer hold a vision of the final object in her mind before production begins, violence in our current moment and for the white middle class arises from a space in which the forethought required by a self-conscious labor process seems increasingly impossible. I will concede that defining violence in this way may seem to give too much to those who would dismiss the desire to produce outside of the established order as irrational. But sometimes there are good—even rational— reasons for pursuing what might at first appear to be irrational courses. For the white middle class (a group for whom imagining consequential action has become increasingly difficult), the "irrational" violence of the first instance is also the point at which it becomes possible to realize that they are capable of meaningful and self-conscious productions.

On this basis, it becomes possible to outline a number of propositions concerning the transformative function of violence. First, because violence is harbinger, it is also precondition. By making genuinely transformative political action thinkable, it allows us to begin treating our psychic addiction to representational proxies. Second, in a unified field, no politics is possible. The supreme ambition of today's society of control has been to render itself homogenous and bereft of tangible exteriorities. Under conditions such as these, violence is required to open up the space for politics. Third, through the force of their assertion and through their confrontation with ruling regimes, activists during the period of anti-globalization struggles began to rediscover the outside.

This "outside" could not be convincingly envisioned in either geographic or spiritual terms. The outside was here. And now. It was waiting to be actualized through production. At its best, the declaration that "another world is possible" was less a form of utopian wish fulfillment than a methodological program for the revitalization of politics in an age when politics itself had been eclipsed by the homogenous continuity of the society of control.

One of the goals of *Black Bloc, White Riot* is to elaborate the concrete process by which these propositions came to be realized.

Throughout the course of this investigation, I've made general use of the term "riot" to denote those open-ended spaces where active experiments with violence became possible. Although many of these encounters would not qualify either legally or by many sociological designations as riots, they nevertheless enabled activists to operate within a fluid and dynamic field in which the connection between production and politics became more explicit. In this sense, they existed on the threshold of a new post-representational moment. Cognizant of the fact that it remains an unconventional usage, I can't envision a better term than "riot" to designate this open-ended field.

And so, while movement actions themselves only occasionally became riots according to conventional definitions, when considered from the standpoint of the ambivalent struggles of the white middle class, it's possible to see how nearly all of these actions had the riot (as I've identified it) as their horizon. This does not mean that all riots (in the legal or sociological sense) are automatically oriented to the post-representational. Indeed, investigations of the history of rioting tend to reveal strange collusions between extra-parliamentary (and extra-legal) measures and the preservation of the representational status quo. Which is to say: historically, the riot has been harnessed to the juggernaut of representational politics just as regularly as it has been unleashed in the interest of producing something new.[9]

Along with this recuperative dynamic, we must also remember that the riot—even in those moments when it exists on the threshold of the post-representational—in and of itself marks only the beginning of unmediated production. This beginning is analytically important; however, it does not exhaust (nor does it even begin to encapsulate) the possibilities denoted by the idea of a revolutionary production. To be sure, riots remain both exhilarating and frightening. However, the very fact that our investigations must continue to attend to them reveals how far we have to go.

■

In Chapter 1, I investigate activist identity as a problem of representation. Media and state efforts to define the contested term "activist" provide a framework in which to learn about how activists envision themselves. A genealogy of the media's "activist" uncovers a highly contradictory identity with deep roots in liberal philosophy and representational politics. Drawing on Dorothy Smith's institutional ethnography, the chapter concludes with an exploration of how the Black Bloc emphasis on "doing" over "meaning" provides a potentially fruitful means of extricating actors from representational constraints.

In Chapter 2, I consider the relationship between direct action and the movement's nascent understanding of the relationship between violence, production, and politics. Anti-globalization activists used direct action to disrupt the status quo. However, while direct action could be used to foster a materialist epistemology concerned with doing, the movement's engagement with direct action often disclosed a residual commitment to idealist thought. Characteristic of this kind of thinking was the tendency to measure an action's success not on the basis of what it concretely produced but on the basis of what it was thought to mean. Drawing on Paulo Freire's discussion of the pedagogical importance of the limit situation and George Smith's writing on political activist ethnography, the chapter concludes with an assessment of the Green Mountain Anarchist Collective's "Communiqué on Tactics and Organization."

In Chapter 3, I explore the difficulties that anti-globalization activists encountered when trying to envision the space of politics. These difficulties were crystallized in the tension between the terms "summit hopping" and "local organizing." Although white middle class activists often opposed summit hopping and advocated local organizing, many found it difficult to envision how they themselves occupied the space of "the local." This difficulty can be attributed to the persistence of the universalizing and transcendental conceits of whiteness and to a corresponding belief in the gross particularity of the Other. Interrogating both the binary opposition between "global" and "local" and the fetishistic elevation of "community" to the position of privileged ground of struggle, I propose that meaningful solidarity between white activists and the communities they designated as "local" demands that white activists become both willing and able to map the specificities of their own situated experiences of globalization. Chapter 3 concludes with a consideration of the Claustrophobia Collective's analysis of the 2001 Cincinnati riots.

In Chapter 4, I explore the gender of violence. Although it was often held to be a site of irredeemable gender exclusion, I demonstrate how the contemporary Black Bloc riot marks the possibility of a post-representational politics pointing beyond "inclusion" and toward the more radical possibility of gender abolition. By reading Black Bloc activity into the history of women's political violence from the middle of the eighteenth century onward, it's possible to see how the anti-globalization riot signaled a break from the representational "politics" that dominated the twentieth century. Drawing on the work of Judith Butler, Laura Riding Jackson, and others, and considering the personal narratives of women who participated in the Black Bloc, I conclude by showing how the modes of post-representational engagement encouraged by Black Bloc rioting might help to inaugurate a mode of politics rooted explicitly in production.

In Chapter 5, I suggest how rioting—despite being an essentially reactive form of activity—allows its participants to concretely prefigure the society they want to create. This is so because the riot yields political subjects that are able to produce the world, subjects that—through the process of transformation the riot entails—are forced to confront the unwritten future within them. From European peasant rebellions to the racial upheavals of nineteenth century America, a genealogy of the riot demonstrates how rioting—whether or not it is carried out in the name of a "progressive" cause—has worked historically to radically transform those who participate. This transformation can be measured by the extent to which participants have been inducted into the field of politics. Although the anti-globalization movement was in many respects a failure, its lasting lesson is this: in late capitalism's endless present, genuine transformation demands that those who have been annexed from the political field find the means of reconnecting with the world lying in wait beyond its representational proxy.

As a coda to the text as a whole, I include an investigation of the relationship between activism and terrorism. Here, I show how, if there is one, the decisive feature of any identity between these two forms of action arises not from their "common" use of violence but rather from their common imbrication in the representational logic of the bourgeois public sphere. From this starting point, I show how, if activists wish to distinguish themselves from terrorists, they must do so by breaking with the spectacular dimensions of contemporary expressive politics. This does not entail a repudiation of violence. On the contrary, it demands that violence be actualized by renewing its bond to production and by emancipating it from the representational domain to which it has been relegated by the spectacle.

■

The anti-globalization movement revealed how, through struggle and violent upheaval, white middle class dissidents could be radically transformed. It also revealed that being true to one's desire is not an easy process. No single act can guarantee it. However, the psychic impossibility of the present has produced a volatile situation. The dirty kids may not have known exactly why they were angry. But this did not prevent them from sensing the danger of not doing anything about it. The issues that compel people to resist globalization—dispossession, the new enclosure, and the militarization of capital—are by now clear. What is often less clear is how these fights also mark an attempt to recover the human soul from the impoverishment it endured the moment it was expelled from the field of politics. For the kids who have everything but feel nothing, there is only one struggle. It is the fight of our lives.

CHAPTER ONE

SEMIOTIC STREET FIGHTS

For many people in Canada and the US, evidence of the anti-globalization movement first took the form of dramatic street-level confrontations that challenged both the ambassadors of neo-liberalism and the police. From smashed Starbucks windows in Seattle[10] to the collapse of the security fence behind which delegates to the Summit of the Americas in Quebec City had hidden,[11] anti-globalization activists gained recognition (and notoriety) through skirmishes with power and the ensuing trail of debris. But alongside these struggles at the barricades, there was another struggle—admittedly less stunning but no less significant.

I am speaking here about the struggle of representation. In the following chapter, I focus on state and media attempts to make sense of the anti-globalization activist between 1999 and the end of 2001. I point out how, for the dissidents involved in these encounters, more than public relations were at stake. Framed by the "Battle of Seattle" and the attack on the World Trade Center, the period of investigation is itself significant. From euphoria to disorientation, these short years marked the movement's abrupt coming of age. Battles over representation—semiotic street fights, as I have called them—were a crucial part of this short history.

Considering state accounts during this period, it's possible to see an obvious attempt to make sense of activists through the framework of criminality and, on occasion, through the lens of "terrorism." Emblematic of these attempts, I focus here on two publicly available Canadian Security Intelligence

Service (CSIS) documents, as well as comments made by Canadian Members of Parliament during debates in the House of Commons. In each case, I point out how, by producing abstract and ideological conceptions of movement participants, these accounts sought to enter *the activist*—rendered as a discrete and transferable conceptual category—into a series of socially coordinated regulatory practices. By generating a specific conceptual content for *the activist*, the state was able to make sense of protest itself through regulatory texts like the Criminal Code of Canada or—in the US—through new "anti-terror" legislation like the USA PATRIOT Act.

The process by which conceptual and textual organization makes criminalization possible is not new. However, the ease with which this was accomplished in the case of anti-globalization struggles highlighted the fragility of activist claims grounded in the representational framework of rights. Representing activists as criminals and security threats (a category that takes on its full significance under the society of control) allowed state actors to initiate legal courses of action designed to more effectively regulate dissent. In the aftermath of September 11, as politicians aimed to extend the scope of "anti-terror" legislation to cover anti-globalization protest scenarios, the fight to add a criminal dimension to representations of *the activist* became increasingly acute.

In order to get a sense of how these new conditions affected movement organizing efforts, it's useful to consider the case of Sherman Austin, the California-based activist whose house was searched by the FBI in January of 2002 under warrant and at gunpoint. His crime? Being connected to raisethefist.org—an activist website onto which a user (who was not Austin) had posted bomb making instructions widely available on the Internet. When Austin traveled to New York for the mass demonstrations against the World Economic Forum one month later, he was immediately picked up by police and brought into custody. In a report for *Z Magazine*, Austin recounts how, "while I was in jail, they handcuffed me and took me to a backroom where a detective from the FBI and a Secret Service agent interrogated me for about three or four hours…"

> During this whole time, I kept noticing more and more FBI agents walking in and out of the room. They asked me stupid questions like whether I was a terrorist or involved in any terrorist organizations. I told them, 'No,' and one of the agents looked at me like I was seriously a terrorist and that I was lying to him. (Frank 2005)

Around the same time, Toronto-based Ontario Coalition Against Poverty (OCAP) organizer John Clarke recounted how he was detained at the Canada-US border while trying to travel to a speaking engagement at the University of Michigan. In a first-person testimonial that circulated widely over the Internet, Clarke recounted how customs officers went about making sense of him. Upon scanning his identification, he quickly became a threat to Homeland Security.

> An officer asked me more questions about my intentions in the US, what anti globalization protests I had attended and whether I opposed the 'ideology of the United States.' My car was searched and I was taken into a room and thoroughly (though not roughly) frisked. I was then told that I would be denied entry to the US and that the FBI and State Department wanted to speak to me.

During his time in custody, Clarke reports how security officials frequently connived to get him to disclose information or to contradict information they already possessed so that they could arrest him. On a number of occasions, their line of questioning pertained to the activities of other high-profile Canadian activists and to the activities of US organizations like the Direct Action Network (DAN). However, it was just when Clarke thought he would be able to leave that things turned truly absurd. "Out of the blue, [the inter-rogator] demanded to know where Osama Bin Laden was hiding. I knew were he was, he insisted. If I grew a beard I would look like Bin Laden. I was holding back on telling him why I was going to the university and who I was going to meet there. If I didn't want to go to jail, it was time to tell him the real story" (Clarke 2002).

Although Austin and Clarke's cases became frequent topics of conversa-tion during this period, their experiences were far from unusual. From the beginning of the anti-globalization movement to its rapid demise, count-less radicals (and many others besides) became familiar with the repressive capacities of state organizations. However, while their experiences were not unique, what Sherman and Clarke's encounters reveal is the willingness of security forces to use the threat of *misrecognition*—a threat that takes as its premise the interchangeability of *activist* and *terrorist*—in order to tighten the screws of regulation. And while it seems unlikely (in these instances) that the conflation was meant to produce anything other than a rupture in otherwise calm demeanors, it is nevertheless evident that the possibility of producing a meaningful conflation has become a valuable asset to the society of control.

In order to make sense of state attempts to represent *the activist* as a criminal or terrorist element, it's useful to consider Dorothy Smith's approach to reading the "ideological" practices of ruling regimes. Ideology, in Smith's sense, is not so much an expression of belief as it is a social practice aimed at abstracting accounts of the world from lived experience and recasting them in a universalized textual domain (1990: 35–36). For instance, by advancing a specific criminal meaning of *the activist* within the law, both CSIS and Canadian politicians have managed to limit the scope of the possible within the realm of dissent. Ideological accounts that make dissident practices recognizable from the standpoint of the conceptual relevancies of the Criminal Code provided the basis for regulatory courses of action.

■

Throughout the course of their semiotic street fights, activists occasionally made efforts to counter state representations that cast them as criminals. Nevertheless, it appears that it has been the institutional ambiguity of the neoliberal state itself that has, to date, posed a much greater obstacle to attempts at regulating protestors through criminalization. In a context where protest is esteemed as a visible expression of democratic rights and freedoms, the attempt to make activists identical to criminals inevitably runs counter to the authenticating gestures of the state. It is therefore not surprising to find figures like Liberal Senator Sharon Carstairs (Manitoba) drawing the distinction between good and bad protestors in no uncertain terms. While bad protestors could not be countenanced, the good protestors—who inadvertently played the role of legitimating supplement—were absolutely indispensable.

During Senate debates immediately following the protests at the Summit of the Americas in Quebec City in April of 2001, Carstairs began by indicating that she thought "the Summit of the Americas was a great success with respect to the manner in which the police forces behaved and with respect to the way in which those individuals who were peaceful demonstrators—and they were by far the vast majority of participants in Quebec City—behaved."

> One very poignant moment for me was when one young student, who clearly was there for peaceful activism, waved his hand to gain the attention of violent protestors and said, "Don't you understand? You are ruining it for the rest of us."[12]

Faced with the improbability of accumulating sufficient political power—at least in the short term—to unsettle judicial and carceral regimes, it's understandable that many anti-globalization activists opted to cast themselves as the "respectable" protestors intended by liberal rights discourse and enshrined in Carstair's comment. However, from the standpoint of movement coherence, this conciliatory strategy had profound consequences. This is so not least because the state seized upon the ambiguities of activist self-identification and subdivided its conceptual categories in order to draw both deeper and more malleable distinctions between the "good" law-abiding protestor and the "bad" terrorist element.

Animated by its own concerns, the state has not always drawn these distinctions in response to activist claims or identity crises. Nevertheless, it's troubling that the organizational nomenclature adopted by activists in one instance can become a policing strategy in the next. During the protests against the Summit of the Americas in Quebec City, organizers divided the demonstration into three separate zones, each designated by a different color (red, yellow, green) and different degree of anticipated confrontation. The zones were created in the interest of making the demonstration as accessible as possible to different kinds of participation. Just over a year later, police at the G8 meeting in Kananaskis, Alberta used this same color code to generate a risk-based taxonomy of troublemakers. Added to the color scheme—and to the top of the list—were the gold-colored terrorists.

It would be one thing if these designations meant that the state aimed to focus its energy on those that the taxonomy deemed threatening. However, since the goal of designation is not so much to recognize as to regulate the designated object, and since state officials reasoned that "terrorists" might embed themselves within the law-abiding crowds of the green zone, it followed that the vigilance of law enforcement officers needed to extend to "good" protestors as well.

Toronto Sun writer Bob MacDonald captured this logic perfectly in "Violence Marches On," a dizzying editorial written just after an OCAP-initiated action aimed at shutting down the Toronto financial district on October 16, 2001. The demonstration, which was called in opposition to the provincial government's war on poor people, proceeded despite widespread uncertainty about the prospects for militant action in the aftermath of September 11. For MacDonald, there was no doubt that dissent was a cover for terror. "The way it works," he pointed out with more than a hint of xenophobia, "is that the demonstrators first simply urge peace and disarmament.

But subsequent 'spontaneous' rallies and demonstrations are joined by more violent elements—perhaps even some Muslim groups" (October 17, 2001). Since violent Muslims might lurk amidst those simply calling for peace, all must be contained.

■

In the media, where the *legal* consequences of representational conflations were less immediate, activists' semiotic struggles had a somewhat different character. Reporters and editors did not concern themselves primarily with entering *the activist* into discourses aimed at the regulation of criminals (although, as MacDonald's comments suggest, it was not beyond some commentators to demand that such criminalization take place). Instead, the dominant ideological practice of media actors (both corporate and "alternative") was to make sense of anti-globalization activists by conceptually rendering them as versions of the incomprehensible other. In this way, these media stories also helped to produce and reinforce a regulatory conception of the law-abiding citizen. This figure has played an important role in the elaboration of the society of control.

As Sherene Razack and others have pointed out, starting in the seventeenth century, the nascent bourgeois states began to produce their idealized schematic counterparts: "the new citizen subject was a figure who, through self-control and self-discipline, achieved mastery over his own body. The self-regulating bourgeois subject had to be spatially separated from the degeneracy, abnormalcy, and excess that would weaken both him and the bourgeois state" (2002: 11). In the present context (a context in which this image of citizenship continues to dominate), it's not surprising that the excessive practices of anti-globalization dissidents put them in danger of being conceptually expelled from the category "citizen."

Media during this period regularly marshaled representational practices ordinarily bound to the histories of scientific rationality and racism. The fact that most anti-globalization activists in Canada and the US were white and bound to social spaces traditionally supported by scientific rationality (such as the university and the suburb) did not prevent media from proceeding in this manner. After all, it was only *the activist* (as abstracted concept) who was under fire in these fights. Perhaps it didn't matter what the activist got up to when she was not being apprehended (whether by police or in news stories) as *the activist*. Wasn't the hope that—like her parents before her (those courageous kids who marched in the sixties)—she would eventually return to the fold?

In order to generate content for their ideological concept, media accounts during this period focused intently upon the *objects* associated with *the activist*. These depictions tended to be overwhelmingly silencing affairs. However, when read symptomatically, there is a great deal that activists can learn from these accounts. In the end, *the activist* described in the media reveals a great deal about both the media and the norms of the society that this media serves and shapes. Cast as an incomprehensible other in need of rationalization and containment, the media's *activist* gives shape to the anxieties of the bourgeois world. And, since activism's objects only acquire commonsense meanings through the power of an orchestrated gaze (and since the media's inventory of activist objects accumulates over time), it's possible to trace a genealogy of bourgeois anxieties by reading activist objects to determine how and when they became meaningful. As new preoccupations overtake older ones; and as older preoccupations manage—in whatever fashion—to be resolved, representations of *the activist* evolve. Finally, when media and state accounts of *the activist* are read together, it becomes possible to trace a loose correspondence between the genealogy of bourgeois anxieties and the evolution of strategies devised to regulate activist excesses.

By tracing how activism's objects become the basis for a stable—if mythic and abstract—identity, and by understanding how these objects become meaningful through the discourses of scientific objectivity and racism, activists could learn how to more effectively challenge the constraints of *activist* identity itself. Developing an understanding of how the representations mobilized in regulatory courses of action are produced is a minimum requirement to developing the capacity to disrupt them. Frequently, however, activists have accepted much of the discursive logic and inherent constraints of media and state accounts. Instead of questioning the legitimacy of a gaze that casts us as violently exterior and binds us to a world of objects, many dissidents have sought to establish their status as "reasonable" beings within the representational sphere.

In the context of expedited criminalization, activist efforts to appear reasonable temporarily yielded some dissidents some breathing room. However, as a strategy, such commitments seem destined to succumb to a law of diminishing returns and "winner loses" failure. Given that media and state representations of *the activist* have been prompted by a global confrontation of divergent interests, the terrain of "the reasonable" will no doubt continue to erode. In the end, what is reasonable to a ruling regime is that which conforms to its interests.

Now fully colonized by managerial and representational techniques of the society of control, the space of "politics" (if it ever was) can no longer be a viable staging ground for consequential disagreement. Under these conditions, dissidents intent on laying purchase to the "reasonable" are left with two options: cease activism (or, at very least, its effective and disruptive practices) or risk criminalization. As US activist Starhawk argued in the wake of massive police repression in Genoa during demonstrations against the G8 in August of 2001, "if this level of repression goes unchallenged, no one is safe, not the most legal NGO, not the most reformist organization with the mildest demands. If we don't act now, when a political space remains open to us, we may lose the space to act at all."[13]

■

In struggles over representations, state and media are, in an ordinary and non-conspiratorial way, motivated by their own institutional interests. We are therefore obliged to ask: what is in the best interests of dissidents? Since this is a strategic question, it's difficult to provide definitive answers. At the very least, however, we would do well to break with the ideological and conceptual practices of the regimes we oppose.[14] Activists could, for instance, develop accounts of activist objects focused less on their implications for identity and more on what these objects *enable*. By recasting objects with an eye toward production rather than representation, activists could begin to devise a genuinely political response.

Since both state and media have seized upon activist identity as a point for the application of regulatory power, it's questionable if activists can gain anything by advancing opposing accounts of *the activist* as noble, heroic, or a good citizen. Nevertheless, this continues to be an overwhelming activist response to vilification. By and large, these efforts have tended to abide by the logic of inversion and conceptual negation—"I know you are but what am I?" Worse than ineffective, activist efforts to determine the content of *activist* have tended inadvertently to reiterate the restrictive epistemic frame of the media and state.

By restricting themselves to answering every charge, dissidents effectively limit themselves to refuting official pronouncements. What our greatest accomplishments make clear, however, is that the course of neo-liberal globalization will be disrupted not with refutations but with a response. As Andrea Nye has pointed out, confrontations with authority that seek to refute its pronouncements happen on the terms set by authority itself. Consequently, even when they are "successful," these confrontations tend to reaffirm the authority of authority. "But if a refutation can always be refuted, a response cuts deeper" (1990: 176). It's therefore significant that, at a critical moment, discussions within the movement (discussions often shaped by the insights of the "bad" protestors) began to reveal attempts to not only refute but also respond to the conceptual practices of ruling regimes.

This threshold was not reached all at once. Depictions of activists became remarkably frequent in popular culture during the first years of the twenty-first century. Even corporations like The Gap found ways of capitalizing on the new renegade mystique. The summer of 2000 witnessed both CTV and CBC television running clips of confrontations between demonstrators and riot cops—squeezed between images of natural disasters and military conflicts—in promotional spots for their news services. More significant than the obvious sensationalism of this Marxploitation, however, was the way these images helped to shape our conception of *the activist* herself. Although the trailers never identified their cast of characters, it was clear that the viewer was supposed to *recognize* who was involved. The rioters were activists. The riot was activism.

Movement participants will object: some might point out that most activism is boring and takes place around tables in dreary rooms at marathon meetings where the most dangerous thing to be confronted is their comrade's coffee breath. Moreover, most people who go to demonstrations never end up clashing with police and those who do tend to represent a very narrow—young, white, middle class and probably male—demographic. Seth Tobocman's account of the struggle to preserve the Lower East Side squats confirms this hunch. According to Tobocman, although media photos usually captured tensions between young white men and police, what these photos neglected to note was that "children, parents and grandparents of all races" were active in the struggle (1999: 318). Nevertheless, these recognizable images come to stand in for actual activists. And, once transposed, *the activist* is news.

If these depictions are pushed to their logical conclusion, we must surmise that activism requires *the activist*—a practitioner bearing an identity. In three seconds of decontextualized footage, television thus turns the world on its head. Although activism denotes an orientation that (by definition) emphasizes productive engagement within the social field, it comes to require *the activist* (an *a priori* conceptual formulation) in order to be made intelligible. No wonder activists have often taken to contesting media depictions.

Inadvertently accepting the logic of media accounts, some have opted to struggle not over the representational transposition of the world but over the content with which *activist* gets filled. This approach is understandable; however, it's a preoccupation that entails a narrowing of the political field. In order to develop a response that's not simply a refutation, it's first necessary to trace the process by which *the activist* is representationally produced.

■

Since identification is a social process, *the activist* (and the associated forms of political regulation) is always in formation. The attributes of the category have been most subject to revision in moments when the character of activism itself has changed. Nevertheless, the period between 1999 and 2001 witnessed the emergence of a series of semi-stable visual codes or "facts" that gave the activist a degree of conceptual stability and coherence. The emergence of these codes allowed the process of *recognizing the activist* to become an ideological practice. According to George Smith, the coordination of "facts" within any discursive regime is subject to the "social organization of the production of the factual account" (1990: 72). In a context where an additive accumulation of coded attributes is taken to imply the presence of a particular subject, the organization of "the facts" enables the ideological moment of recognition. Within a textually mediated relation of ruling, recognition initiates a course of action aimed at organizing and regulating lived actuality. This general account of the process of recognition-inscription has serious practical implications for activists.

For instance, while anti-globalization activists may have held a variety of beliefs about what they were doing, their characterization by CSIS as a "security threat" prompted courses of action that extended far beyond the framework of these self-perceptions. In this case, the course of action brought about by "recognizing" the "security threat" included reporting "the threat" to the government so that they could make appropriate institutional decisions. From there, the government could pass new legislation aimed at dealing with the problem. This legislation is made coherent through "the facts" produced and compiled by CSIS.

Under the "Reporting Responsibilities" section of their 2000 Public Report, we learn that "the primary mandate of CSIS is to collect and analyze information, *and to report to and advise the government of threats to the security of Canada*... [A]nalysts use their knowledge of regional, national and global trends to assess the quality of information gathered, and to organize it into useful security intelligence products." In this way, the organization of "the facts" helps to *produce* and *organize* the reality it merely claims to describe. But "a fact's organization of actuality is not simply the expectation of an order already perceived," Smith argues. Rather,

> A fact is constructed in a definite institutional context, and its organization reflects that context. An inner coherence is established between the actuality thus represented and the statements that can be made about it, such that the actuality, produced as "what actually happened/what is," can be seen to require its own descriptive categories and conceptual procedures. (1990: 78)

Institutionally committed to factual accounts called "news," media have been as actively involved in the conceptual production of *the activist* as has the state. Reading these accounts symptomatically allows us to discern the logic and conceptual organization of their production. Unfortunately, despite yielding knowledge that could counter the regulatory strategies aimed at our domestication, analyzing the production of factual accounts has not yet become the primary means by which activists make sense of (or challenge) media representations. In fact, for the most part, dissidents continue to consider their own activities in representational rather than productive terms.

■

"Hell No, We Won't Show!" screamed the anti-protest headline in *The Excalibur*, York University's student paper. Accompanying the June 7, 2000 editorial was a cartoon entitled "The Modern Protester" (Figure 1). Standing in the middle of an otherwise empty frame (lacking even a horizon line), *Excalibur's Modern Protestor* looked like a biology specimen. Indeed, the diagram was labeled, arrows pointing here and there to important aspects of the object under consideration. With great care, the artist highlighted kneepads ("protection from asphalt when brute force is applied"), a gas mask ("protection from tear gas and pepper spray"), a helmet ("protection from nightstick blows to the head"), and a bulletproof vest ("protection from crossfire and stray bullets").

What are we to make of this schematic organization of "the facts" of *The Modern Protestor*? Blatant to the point of absurdity, it is nevertheless worth noting that this schematic mode of representation derives from the gaze perfected by scientific objectivity. Through a process of visual schematization, *The Modern Protestor* in this organization of "the facts" becomes an object to

Figure 1: "The Modern Protester"
The Excalibur June 7, 2000 p. 6

be considered. Indeed, the status of *The Modern Protestor* is established (and determined) by the objects with which it has been associated.

Through *The Excalibur* cartoon, *The Modern Protestor* becomes a monster;[15] a subject whose subjectivity is merely an aspect of the object considered; a subject who, like a specimen, can literally be dissected by the scientific gaze. In the end, *The Modern Protestor* becomes a concept, a character without a history, a personality, or a voice. This description should not be taken to imply a particular injury. As far as slander goes, *The Excalibur* cartoon is a relatively minor affair. Nevertheless, the depiction is significant because of its explicit effort to objectify the subject in order to make sense of (and thus contain) the indeterminacies brought about by *The Modern Protestor*'s arrival on the scene. Considered from this vantage, it's especially significant that this process of categorical elaboration took place in a campus newspaper. Because campuses were important organizational nodes within the early phase of the movement, it's not surprising that students on both Left and Right engaged in ad-hoc and everyday attempts to solidify coherent conceptions.

Visual representations of bodies played a central role in this process. Here, the term "representation" needs to be understood not only as a process of content selection but also as a *technique*, a method by which the selected content becomes intelligible. To see this process at work, it's useful to consider Richard Dyer's account of the relationship between whiteness and photography. According to Dyer (1997: 108–115), the historic elaboration of photographic and lighting techniques served to representationally elevate the white bourgeois subject. At the same time, racialized subject-objects (along with subject-objects from the working class) tended instead to be *possessed* by it. Although achieved through the mobilization of a different technical repertoire, possession through representational means is also readily apparent when we consider the implications of *The Excalibur*'s depiction of *The Modern Protestor*.

■

By looking at objects and the meanings attributed to them at any given moment, we run the risk of missing how these objects have been characterized over time and in other contexts. It's worth considering, then, how many of *Excalibur*'s objects—cast in the illustration as "protection"—have been described elsewhere in the media as *weapons*. Somewhat more charitable, I don't take *Excalibur*'s framing to mean that they opted, in this instance, to be on our side. Considered as part of a social process still unfolding, the discrepancy between representations that classified activist gear as protection and those that cast it as weaponry is best understood as a skirmish over signifiers to which no common meaning had yet been affixed. Although, over the past decade, these objects have come to have a stable referent, things were still up in the air when *The Excalibur* cartoon first appeared in 2000.

At stake in these different characterizations is the definition of the concept *activist*. What will the content of this term be? Is *The Modern Protestor* a citizen trying to assert the right to protest despite the unfortunate cloud of tear gas or is she a menace with malice on the brain? With obvious legal implications, this debate was of concern to many civil libertarians. Pointing out the evident contradictions at play in attempts to cast activist objects as weapons, Ruckus Society activist John Sellers lamented how, in the United States at the beginning of the twenty-first century, "you can drive around with an AK-47 but not a couple of plastic tubes that you might use in a non-violent protest."

Writing in *This Magazine*, JB MacKinnon explains that Sellers was referring to "the so-called 'sleeping dragons' used to cover protestors' linked or locked arms in a direct action blockade." With evident bemusement, MacKinnon recounted how "in Washington DC, during the IMF-World Bank meeting, carrying sleeping dragons or even art supplies became an excuse to stop, seize and arrest" (2000: 29). Consequently, activists began hiding their blockade materials (Trojan Horse-style) inside the frames of street puppets. Concerned with maintaining the element of surprise, the activist use of street puppets also amounted to a semiotic street fight of the first order. Sellers himself became the object of a semiotic street fight when he was arrested during demonstrations against the Republican National Convention in Philadelphia in 2000 and released on a bail of US $1 Million.

A few months after A16, concerned citizen Ian Brown wrote a letter to the *Toronto Star* confirming that protective protest gear was indeed best understood as weaponry. Commenting on the decorum of protestors at an

OCAP-led demonstration at Queen's Park on June 15, 2000, Brown argued that demonstrators "would not arrive at the protest in balaclavas, gas masks and goggles, dressed for war rather than discussion" if their intentions had been honorable (June 21, 2000). Called to demand redress for a litany of injustices endured by poor people,[16] the demonstration involved nearly 2000 participants and ended in a massive altercation with police. In both legal and media accounts, the event quickly became a "riot."

Representing the demonstration as a riot was important to Crown attorneys who used the designation to make their case. Since police charged most of those arrested—more than fifty in total—with counts of "participating in a riot," any uncertainty about whether or not the label could be properly applied would have been extremely harmful. But even though many of the charges were eventually thrown out of court precisely on the grounds that it was not clear that the label "riot" applied, it did not take long for June 15 to become a riot in the social imaginary. Reiterating the logic that insists protestors ought to occupy the moral high ground, Brown concluded his letter to *The Star* by indicating that, despite having been brutally beaten by police on that day, demonstrators "should have shouted 'Shame, shame' at themselves."

Accompanying Brown's letter, *The Star* ran a photo of a tattooed white protestor wearing a gas mask and bandana. Over the next couple of years, images such as this one featured prominently in media accounts of activists. And while the meaning of objects like *the gas mask* remained a contested matter,[17] these objects nevertheless become recognized signifiers of a new generation of resistance. But photojournalists were not the only ones drawn to these signifiers. In the lead up to the protests against the Summit of the Americas in Quebec City, activists released promotional materials bearing the image of an iconic gas mask along with text that read "Quebec City: The Most Fun You've Had Since Seattle."

Semiotic street fights of this kind suggest that it's been relatively easy for activists to challenge (or at least ridicule) the regulatory claims of media and state bodies. However, it has remained far more difficult for us to recognize our own imbrication in the representational sphere. Here, in the realm of conceptual action where engagement at the level of the signifier makes the possibility of engaging at the level of the signified fall from view, activists have often ended up silently adopting the conceptual relevancies of their opponents. Given the extent to which police and politicians have managed to force a correspondence between *activist* and *terrorist*—if not yet in the courts then at least in the social imaginary—this collusion is especially troubling.

■

As anti-globalization protests escalated in frequency and—on occasion—in intensity, state and police agencies began to reorganize the "facts" of activism. Facilitated by a series of semiotic contortions, the new state facticity attempted to recast *The Modern Protestor* as a terrorist class. Police commissioner John Timoney, who oversaw the police operation at protests against the 2000 Republican National Convention in Philadelphia, played a central role in this transposition. Describing the movement in the summer of 2000, Timoney recounted how "there's a cadre, if you will, of criminal conspirators who are about the business of planning conspiracies to go in and cause mayhem and property damage and violence in major cities in America" (Ferguson 2000: 50). Especially since September 11, it's clear how closely this account anticipates and reiterates the conceptual content of *terrorist*. However, while it was amplified by the "war on terror," this conflation has much deeper roots.

According to MacKinnon, although "progressives recoil at the thought that they could be seen as a threat on par with the Yankee militias," they nevertheless find themselves designated by a common nomenclature. "The word 'terrorist'," MacKinnon reminds us, "has been readily applied to animal-rights activists who release mink from fur farms, eco-saboteurs who damage logging equipment, and certainly to anyone who wears a balaclava." This list is striking because of the ease with which the actions described in the first two instances devolve seamlessly into an account of an *object*—the balaclava—in the last. Here, the object itself invokes terror. As far as MacKinnon is concerned, the conflation between *progressives* and *terrorists* is patently ridiculous. "For a taste of how absurdly far-fetched perceptions of leftist activism can be," he proposes, "consider a column by journalist and self-declared espionage expert Paul Jackson in the May 2 issue of the *Calgary Sun*."[18]

> "How is it that these supposedly motley crews—looking like the disorganized flotsam and jetsam of the world's radical left—can be so well organized?" asks Jackson. Jackson has his theory. He sees "three immediate possibilities" behind the Left's capacity to select targets, book accommodations and organize such effective dissent: Moammar Gadhafi of Lybia, Saddam Hussein of Iraq, and Osama bin Laden of Afghanistan. (MacKinnon 2000: 29)

Although the anti-globalization movement in Canada and the US was comprised overwhelmingly of white activists, this did not prevent media commentators from drawing on racist anxieties to undermine its efforts. This was possible in part because, as Joy James has pointed out, the image of the international security threat—a designation applied to anti-globalization protestors and terrorists alike—has been Middle Eastern (1997: 107). Insinuations that America's Middle Eastern "enemies" were behind anti-globalization protests are, of course, spurious. However, this has not prevented various anti-movement actors from trying to benefit from the conflation.

For instance, in October of 2001, executive director of B'nai Brith Canada Frank Dimant held a press conference condemning the radical Concordia Student Union for its student handbook entitled *Uprising*. Released just prior to September 11 and including content that fused anti-globalization sentiments with active support for the liberation of Palestine, the handbook was denounced by Dimant in terms that actively conflated radicals with terrorists. "Is this a blueprint for Osama bin Laden's youth program in North America," he asked rhetorically. If it wasn't already clear, the absurdity of Dimant's question becomes explicit when one considers *Uprising*'s unapologetically queer and feminist content.

But beyond the racism implicit in state and media discussions of "international security threats," there are two features of Jackson and MacKinnon's words—and the interaction between them—that deserve comment. The first is that it was possible for Jackson to have made his claim in the first place. The second is that, in countering this absurdity, MacKinnon elected to advance an *alternate representation*. The problem is "resolved" by changing the content assigned to the signifier. Although protestors sometimes look scary, they are not *really* a threat—at least not one on par with Middle Eastern terrorists. Whether or not it was deliberate, MacKinnon ends up binding the activist to state-fostered conceptions of the good concerned citizen, the reasonable rights-bearing subject of liberalism.

Given MacKinnon's evident sympathies with the activist cause, perhaps this is reasonable. A cursory glance at a CSIS report issued in 2000, for instance, presents a vision of anti-globalization activism that indeed looks threatening. It's a vision that any strategically sensible movement advocate would seek to refute. MacKinnon's comments might therefore be best read as recognition of the consequences of being labeled a "security threat." Perhaps he decided—in a moment of shrewd calculation—that such a classification was more heat than the movement could afford.

Indeed, being an international security threat is a precarious undertaking. CSIS's list of turn-of-the-century threats to the "global security environment" is truly astounding. Along with the rise of international terrorist networks, CSIS expressed concern that some members of "Canada's ethnic communities" felt implicated in and connected to "violent foreign conflicts." Additionally, they expressed concern over the related matters of proliferating "weapons of mass destruction" and the threat of retaliation against Canada for its role in "resolving foreign conflicts." Rounding off their list of global threats, CSIS enumerated various regional conflicts including the struggle between Palestinians and Israelis, ongoing "tensions" in Yugoslavia, skirmishes between India and Pakistan over Kashmir, and the ongoing "troubles" in Northern Ireland.

At the bottom of this impressive list of security threats, CSIS includes the rise of the anti-globalization movement. Last, but definitely not least, the document devotes four whole paragraphs to the threat posed by activists. Considering the single paragraph summaries allotted to each of the other important international conflicts cited in the document, the extensive account of the summit hoppers seems especially notable. According to CSIS, the anti-globalization movement was composed of activists "representing a broad spectrum of groups, lobbyists and overlapping networks, including a limited number of violent extremists."

> [These groups] share a mutual antipathy for multinational corporate power. Large corporations with international undertakings stand accused of social injustice and unfair labour practices, as well as a lack of concern for the environment, mismanagement of natural resources and ecological damage... Underlying the anti-globalization theme is criticism of the capitalist philosophy, a stance promoted again by left-of-centre activists and militant anarchists... Circumstances have also promoted the involvement of fringe extremists who espouse violence, largely represented by *Black Bloc* anarchists and factions of militant animal rights and environmental activists. (CSIS 2000b)

It's worth considering how, if it were not for a fundamental conflict of interests, CSIS's description of "activist traits" might be mistaken for a list of admirable qualities to which every citizen should aspire. Listen, for instance, to this benign description of our "threatening" practices:

> [Using the Internet,] individuals and groups are able to identify and publicize

targets, solicit and encourage support, establish dates, recruit, raise funds, share experiences, accept responsibilities, arrange logistics, and promote goals... (2000b)

Although they might easily be mistaken for provisions in the mandate of the local Rotary Club, these were the practices that turned anti-globalization activists into threats to international security. It's not surprising, then, that CSIS identified its inability to "legally" eavesdrop on online discussions as a principle barrier to its capacity to respond in a timely fashion to the shifting security environment. Moreover, since the violent extremists in the movement (a movement that—after all—was nothing more coherent than a series of "overlapping networks") could be anywhere, the movement as a whole needed to be increasingly scrutinized.

After September 11, these themes were extensively discussed in the House of Commons. During debates about Bill C-36 (Canada's widely criticized replica of the USA PATRIOT Act), Liberal MP John Bryden defended the legislation despite legitimate fears that it would infringe upon civil liberties and the right to dissent. In his estimation, the Bill needed to be broad enough to encapsulate anti-globalization protests. "What choice do we have," he asked.

These are not peaceful protests we are dealing with. We are dealing with violent protests and it becomes increasingly dangerous to have any kind of international conference... [A]s long as protestors are allowed to wear masks, as long as they use violence and as long as there is a chance that terrorists may be infiltrating such protestors wearing masks, I do not know what choice we have but to give the RCMP reasonable powers to bring peace to protestors. (Hansard, Nov 29: 2001)

Forget, if you can, that the only group ever commonly acknowledged to have infiltrated a group of protestors wearing masks were police who, during the G8 Summit in Genoa, donned Black Bloc gear and proceeded as *agents provocateurs*. Since *terrorist* and *activist* correspond to discrete courses of action within the law and the social imaginary, the semiotic exchange of *terrorist* for *activist* has become a justification for increased repression. And while activists, social movement theorists, and media and state agencies have all expressed disagreements about the meaning of *the activist*, it's clear that—since September 11—the meaning of terror has been severely truncated.

The question, of course, is not whether the state and media actually believe that contemporary activists harbor terrorist capacities. Whether they are using mere hyperbole to engender desirable social responses or are shaking in their boots, it's evident that what's being sought is not clarity but justification. At the same time, the associative strategy that makes sense of *the activist* through the more established signifier *terrorist* also denotes a reorganization of the "facts." In this way, *the activist* becomes a residual category, a symptom of the bourgeois world. A genealogy of representations of *the activist* thus allows us to see how anti-globalization struggles also transformed those they opposed.

■

Media depictions of anti-globalization activists in the period after Seattle prominently displayed the gear featured in the *Excalibur* cartoon. But while they became everyday referents, it's important to consider how, even three months prior to Seattle, these objects would not (indeed, could not) have been the defining features of activist representation. Before Seattle, depictions of the genealogical precursors to *The Modern Protestor* relied on a different series of signifiers. Just beneath the debates about the offensive or defensive character of *The Modern Protestor*'s equipment lies a whole genealogy, a series of points plotted along the axis of recognition. And while they do not necessarily evoke legal considerations in the same way, they are nevertheless important dimensions of the identity under consideration. Who was this activist before she became a criminal, a terrorist, a threat to international security?

Looking at representations rendered prior to Seattle, it's possible to see just how quickly the ordering of the facts of activism can shift. But even depictions rendered during the period under consideration reveal how the contested signifiers are piled onto a series of sedimented and taken-for-granted visual cues that are no longer called into question. Even in *The Excalibur* cartoon, just beneath the level of active signification, a whole genealogy unfolds. What do we learn about *The Modern Protestor* by investigating the parts of the drawing that aren't labeled? Reading the visual cues that, in the estimation of the artist, did not need comment, it's possible to unearth some of the now commonsensical assumptions that give content to the category *activist*.

Excalibur's *Modern Protestor* is highly androgynous, although would most likely be read as male. And white. Of the clothing that has not been labeled, there are heavy black shoes or boots and extremely baggy pants held up with a utility belt. His coat has large pockets and hangs loosely around modest and slightly slouched shoulders. Poking through the straps of his gas mask are tufts of spiky hair. The requisite backpack hangs from his frame. As is now customary, his pants rest about six inches below his waist. Although all of these signifiers have discrete social origins, they have—through a process of sedimentation—become indistinguishable from the category *activist* itself. They did not deserve comment.

Figure 1: "The Modern Protester"   Figure 2: "The Face of Protest"
The Excalibur, June 7, 2000: p. 6   *The Globe and Mail*, June 5, 2000: p. A1

That the production of meaning is a social and historical process that relies on the circulation and repetition of ordered signifiers is unquestionable. *The Modern Protestor* appeared in *The Excalibur* on June 7, 2000 as part of an issue devoted to coverage of the "Shut Down the OAS" demonstrations that took place in Windsor the previous weekend. In nearly every respect, *Excalibur's* "protestor" looks virtually identical to an actual photograph of a demonstrator from Windsor that appeared just two days earlier in *The Toronto Sun, The Globe and Mail*, and *The Windsor Star* (Figure 2). On the cover of *The Globe and Mail*, the photo was accompanied by a caption that identified the demonstrator as "The Face of Protest" (June 5, 2000: A1).

Apart from the obvious physical similarities, both figures—*The Face of Protest* and *The Modern Protester*—are characterized as definitive types. That their appearances are so congruent suggests that this "type" had, by the summer of 2000, effectively entered into wide circulation within the symbolic economy. Given the timing of the image's appearance, it's likely that *The Excalibur* artist referenced the Canadian Press photo (though the similarity would be all the more remarkable if they hadn't). As a moniker, *The Face of Protest* served both to individuate the social act of protest—thus rendering it as identity—and to enact a process of selection and repetition that effectively codified meaning. From here, *the activist* was free to circulate as an abstract category bound within the rigid frame of socially organized processes of recognition.

■

Although only some of *The Modern Protestor*'s belongings were labeled, consideration of the entire image yields clues to the process of meaning-making that accompanied the anti-globalization activist's rise to recognition. And while the duly noted signifiers added to an evolving definition of protest, the sub-cultural cues that were not commented upon (the ones that could be assumed by both illustrator and reader) must also be considered. As elements of the anti-globalization *activist*'s representational prehistory, they are an important part of the story. And they point back much further than might at first be imagined.

On September 14, 1999, Concordia University's student paper *The Link* printed a cartoon field guide for "how to spot activists" on campus. Under the banner "*The Link*'s Activist Toolbox: Everything You Need to Know to Be a Dissident in Montreal" was an illustration drawn to resemble a paper doll cut-out activity set. "Build your own activist," invited the cartoon (Figure 3). Accompanying the drawing, *The Link* printed the following explanation: "Concordia activists are a special breed. In case you haven't been able to pick them out already, this custom designed paper doll set should help you out. Feel free to cut and paste accessories, or even draw your own." While this approach to representation is far more novel than the specimen-like illustration featured in *The Excalibur*, it nevertheless shares the same epistemic premise. Through a process of objectification and discrete labeling, the viewer is encouraged to recognize *the activist*.

Avoiding practices—those things that put the "active" in activism—the cartoon proceeds instead through a taxonomic

Figure 3: Graham and Troster, "Build Your Own Activist"
The Link, September 14, 1999: p. 6

catalogue of objects. Amongst *the activist*'s "accessories" are bicycles, bongo drums, organic soymilk, and spray paint. For clothing, the two models—one male, one female, both apparently white, standing around in their underwear in a state of comfortable androgyny—are provided with heavy boots, large heavy army pants with multiple pockets and t-shirts bearing political slogans and the names of organizations. "Food Not Bombs" reads one, "Fuck Suharto" exclaims the other. Aesthetically, these clothes bear a remarkable similarity to those worn by *Excalibur*'s *Modern Protestor*. Other accessories available to these cut and paste creations: a portable radio and a tape by Propagandhi (identified as "good news" punk music), a keeper,[19] and—perhaps most significant—two halos graced with the text "keen awareness of white male privilege."

Drawn nearly a year earlier, "Concordia's special breed" is undeniably a genealogical precursor to *The Modern Protestor*. By the time *Excalibur* got around to it, the aesthetic highlighted in *The Link* cartoon could be assumed.

But where did *The Link*'s signifiers come from? A closer investigation reveals an intriguing genealogical inheritance. Although the artist did not comment upon it, Concordia's "special breed" appears to draw deeply from the river of Christianity before following it downstream to the nineteenth century estuary of romantic liberalism. Along with Propagandhi's "good news," the analogy drawn between saintliness and awareness of white male privilege confirms the artist's recourse to the Christian archive. Following a convention that identifies resistance as the radical negation of that which it opposes, *The Link* treats awareness as a return—or elevation—to innocence. Here, while the reference was not likely deliberate, the depiction ends up reiterating prominent themes from the romantic tradition.

For instance, Henry David Thoreau thought that withdrawal of consent—pure negation—was tantamount to an assertion of glorious individual will. In *Civil Disobedience*, Thoreau assigns the task of renouncing the government to a group he calls *men*. But *men* who resist, in Thoreau's account, are ontologically distinct from those too closely bound to the state—that is, all other men who, despite being conceptual equivalents, are incapable of resistance. Soldiers, constables, jailers, and lawyers: Thoreau casts them all under suspicion. "The mass of men serve the state," he writes, "not as men mainly, but as machines, with their bodies."

> They are the standing army, and the militia, jailers, constables, *posse comitatus*, etc. In most cases there is no free exercise whatever of the judgement or of the moral sense; but they put themselves on a level with wood and earth

and stones; and wooden men can perhaps be manufactured that will serve the purpose as well. Such command no more respect than men of straw or a lump of dirt. They have the same sort of worth only as horses and dogs. Yet such as these are even commonly esteemed good citizens... A very few—as heroes, patriots, martyrs, reformers in the great sense, and men—serve the state with their consciences also, and so necessarily resist it for the most part; and they are commonly treated as enemies by it. (1960: 237)

So, while resistance requires *men*, Thoreau is convinced that "the mass of men serve the state." Because of this, resistance becomes an elevated calling, a kind of devotional act carried out by those who are able to make moral distinctions and thus to serve God/the state. In the process of defining themselves in opposition to the dominant order and becoming "martyrs," subjects who resist through the withdrawal of consent advance for themselves a heroic, messianic ontology; it is a state made possible by the belief that they are not that which they resist. Even though, as ontological equivalents, all *men* are capable of resistance, only a precious few actually resist. Through the act of conscience, Thoreau's resistant *men* elevate themselves above all others; and these others fall to earth, cast aside like "a lump of dirt." Concordia's "special breed," halo firmly on head, confirms this legacy.

According to Dyer, ontological conceptions that enable us to draw distinctions between equivalent forms have been pivotal to the emergence and historical elaboration of whiteness. Starting with the Christian notion of *spirit* (that thing which is *in* but not *of* the body) and secularized as the transcendent within continental philosophy, white ontology has been indelibly marked by anxiety-producing becoming. To use Thoreau's example, the inevitable question posed by whiteness is thus: are we men, or are we *men*? For this reason, whiteness encounters its nervous condition at precisely the point where its devotees realize that, if the process of becoming ceases, they might disappear for good. And so they keep moving.

Restless, the white subject's productivity arises from the fact that it's ontologically impossible for him to sit still. And is this not the case for activists as well? Anxious productivity, activism's nervous condition: it's hard not to perceive the bastard inversion of transcendental white ontology permeating activist culture. And it's on this basis that we can make sense of the frequent— though frequently unconscious—Christological citations in activist texts. How else are we to understand the aesthetic decisions that framed the image of John Clarke shot on the day of the Queen's Park riot and published in

Figure 4: John Clarke   Figure 5: Duccio di Buoninsegna,
June 15, 2000. Photo by David Maltby   "The Way to Calvary" (1308–11)

Now Magazine? In a remarkable instance of citation without quotation marks, the image perfectly reiterates—and thus becomes infused with the affective weight of—the devotional posture and situational iconography of Italian proto-Renaissance artist Duccio di Buoninsegna's "Way to Calvary" (1308–11).

■

While there may be a connection between white activists and a discrete world of objects which, when taken collectively, might be recognizable as a coherent aesthetic or identity, this connection can't simply be understood through the logic of signification. To break with the conceptual practices of media and state, activists need to devise another approach to the question of representation and another strategy for apprehending our objects. The importance of reading objects in their historical-relational dynamism becomes evident in moments of danger. To get a sense of this process, it's useful to turn once again to the past in the hope of uncovering another—more productive—genealogical current running through contemporary activist practice. Specifically, it's useful to consider Joan of Arc's decision to wear male clothing.

"Essentially seen as a transvestite by scholars and artists who came after her and took her as a subject," says Andrea Dworkin, "Joan's defiance, her rebellion, is trivialized as a sexual kink, more style than substance, at most an interesting wrinkle in a psychosexual tragedy of a girl who wanted to be a boy and came to a bad end." In Dworkin's estimation, "romantics, especially the filmmakers, seem to see the male clothing as an esthetic choice, the beauty of her androgyny highlighted by the graceful boylike look." But this preoccupation with the signifier ends up concealing what is most important:

> The clothes made her life of high adventure and martial brilliance possible; she needed them, a sword, a horse, a banner, a king, a cause, all of which she got with an intransigence that is the mark of genius. The male clothing—*the signifier and the enabler*, signifying rebellion, enabling action—became the emblem of a distinct integrity for those who hated her. (1987: 100, italics mine)

With perhaps less heroic impulses, similar patterns could be faintly traced in the clothing and object choices of anti-globalization activists. Activist feet *were* often bound in heavy boots; pants and shirts *did* get borrowed from the wardrobe of blue-collar work. On some, hardware began to appear. Pockets for knives, screwdrivers, and especially big black markers grew like tumors on people's pants. Every surface became a space from which to pronounce political messages.

Perhaps the most commented-upon piece of this new activist "uniform" was the hooded sweatshirt. Indigenous to both punk rock and hip hop (but popularized by the latter), the hoodie was often described as the perfect synthesis of functionality and a militant aesthetic. In a compare-and-contrast essay on police and protestor gear—provocatively entitled "Who's the Thug?"—*Now Magazine* writer Nabil Elsaadi championed the hoodie in a manner consistent with Dworkin's analysis of Joan of Arc. For Elsaadi, activist hoodies were "tear gas protection and fashionable too" (Elsaadi 2001: 19). Forgetting for the moment that a hoodie affords little protection from tear gas, we are left with an object perceived as both signifier and enabler.

In the context of the anti-globalization movement, which (on occasion) sidestepped legality in order to be effective, the emphasis on the enabling is especially significant. Without foreclosing discussion about the potential significance of the glamour of resistance, it seems clear that—in order to be effective—activists need to reconnect with the realm beyond (or beneath) the signifier.

Can activists begin to conceive of our objects in such a way that they highlight social relations and the means by which they can be transformed? Given the extent to which activist representation has been put to the service of regulation, this would be a welcome possibility. It's useful here to draw upon the insights of an unlikely couple—the "militant anarchists" feared by CSIS and that old curmudgeon, Karl Marx. According to Bertell Ollman, Marx's principal contribution to understanding historical processes was his ability to perceive *objects* as *relations* (1971: 27). An object, Marx proposed, contained traces of everything that went into its realization. And, since objects were fleeting fixities (temporary traces of ongoing human activity), their present shape could not be taken to be their timeless substance or truth.

Perceived in this manner, objects become a symptom of the social relations that heralded their emergence. Individual objects, when apprehended relationally, therefore become important points of entry into an understanding of the whole to which they are bound. According to Ollman, Marx devised his understanding of this relational dynamic through a critical reading of German idealist philosophy and (in particular) the work of Hegel, who threw the very notion of identity into question. "In establishing the identity of each thing in its relation to the whole, as a mode of expression of the Absolute," Ollman writes, "Hegel altered the notion of identity used by Kant and of truth itself."

> Mathematical equality (1=1) is replaced as the model for comprehending identity by what might be called 'relational equality,' where the entity in question is considered identical with the whole that it relationally expresses. (1971: 33)

Although Marx rebelled against Hegel's idealism, he never disavowed his account of the relational dynamism of the world. Following Marx, Ollman suggests that the connections between things are best understood not as logical relations but as *ontological* ones (1971: 34). Whereas idealist thought plots relationships of abstract causality (a process clearly at work in MP Bryden's assertion that mask-wearing protestors provide cover for terrorists), the process of apprehending activist objects through their ontological relationality allows us to consider them as expressions of the contradictions at work within the social whole. Here, objects disclose their use-value and their enabling potential, and can be approached productively. The signifier gives way to the signified.

■

In and of itself, philosophical hairsplitting of this kind is unlikely to be of any use. Still less will it be appealing to many who were counted amongst the movement's "violent extremists." Nevertheless, it's interesting to note the regularity with which challenges to the limits of idealist thought and conceptual "action" appear in their statements. Speaking, for instance, of the importance of wearing masks at demonstrations, an activist writing on infoshop.org advanced the following proposition:

> Wearing masks is such an effective tactic that more and more police departments are implementing anti-mask laws. The practice of "masking up" is controversial within activist circles. Some activists criticize mask-wearing because it contradicts the image of activism being open and accessible, in other words, "we have nothing to hide." There are several reasons for wearing masks at an action: 1) to protect ourselves from illegal police surveillance; 2) to promote anonymity among the ranks, which helps protect against the rise of charismatic leaders; 3) to provide cover for activists engaged in illegal actions during the demo, and 4) to promote solidarity within the bloc. (infoshop.org, 2001)

By speaking about what the mask *enables* and not what it *means*; by not seeking to simply refute possible negative readings (for instance, the suggestion that the mask contradicts the idea that activists have nothing to hide), the Black Bloc statement effectively reformulates the relationship between activists and objects. Rather than asserting an abstract right to wear masks, these activists proceeded instead by taking legal regulation as one variable among others within a mobile terrain of struggle. In short, the Black Bloc orientation to masks suggests the concrete means by which representation is supplanted by production. And, since what the Black Bloc wants to produce (as can be adduced from the passage above) is clearly at odds with the wishes of the state, it marks a preliminary moment in the elaboration of a genuinely political opposition. From the managerial realm of surveillance and the bio-political possession of the body comes the mask. By wearing it, the activist enabled her passage through violence from ontology to politics.

When considered as an aspect of the overall anti-globalization project, the question of masks remained a relatively small matter. Corporate globalization was not halted; activists in balaclavas did not manage to turn the world upside down. What remains significant about the mask, however, is what it suggests about the prerequisites for political being. If contemporary activists hope to build upon the initial successes of this period, it will be important for us to continue developing an understanding of social relations that breaks with the conceptual mystifications of representation. In Chapter 2, I will explore how direct action has and can be used as a weapon in this war.

CHAPTER TWO

DIRECT ACTION, PEDAGOGY OF THE OPPRESSED

O n September 27, 2002, thousands of activists from across the United States descended on Washington, DC to challenge the increasing barbarity of the neo-liberal world. In what was to be the first major convergence of anti-globalization and anti-war sensibilities post September 11, the People's Strike—as the day was called—targeted both US imperialist military policy and the IMF/World Bank leviathan. As with previous mass demonstrations in DC, activists were confronted with sweeping arrests. Among those picked up and detained were three women who, in the spirit of non-cooperation that had become a cornerstone of movement activity since Seattle, chose to delay and frustrate the state's attempt to process them by refusing to provide identification. Since the police could not process them at the station and since they could not be released on bail, the Jane Does, as the activists came to be known, were transferred to a Washington-area women's prison.

As might be expected, this change of venue led the organizers of the People's Strike—DC's Anti-Capitalist Convergence (ACC)—to begin coordinating jail visits. Within a few days, their efforts led them to circulate instructions for how to visit the Jane Does over the Internet. Jails, after all, have rules and, if activists were to be able to visit their comrades, they would have to know how to approximate good behavior. Presumably because of the prison policies they had encountered, the ACC posted the following "rules for visits" on their website: "30 minutes for each visit, only 2 adults at a time, No sandals or open-toed shoes. No sweat suits, No camouflage, No cross-dressing. Women must (appear to be) wearing a bra." To the end of these regulations, ACC added the following parenthetic note: "(Unfortunately, this is not a joke)." Indeed.

While the bemusement is noteworthy, I think the encounter with prison regulations described above has significance beyond providing another anecdotal basis for despising institutional (hetero)sexism. Apart from the offensive, decidedly unfunny, encounter with antiquated gender categories, what took place in this interaction? Through what process did ACC activists come to know prison visit rules? In order to answer these questions, it's useful to consider how direct action and confrontation allowed these activists to learn something very concrete about the belly of the beast.

Many anti-globalization activists embraced direct action as an effective means of struggle. What was less frequently considered, however, was how direct action might also be the basis for a new kind of thinking. By reading the movement's direct action practices through the insights of radical educator Paulo Freire and activist-scholar George Smith, it becomes clear that direct action is more than an effective and courageous means of resistance; it can be a potentially effective research practice and pedagogy as well. However, a sober assessment of the movement's direct action practices also reveals how residual commitments to forms of idealist thought (forms of thinking that emphasize the signifier over the signified and confuse representation with production) currently make it all the more difficult for us to make the most of this potential.

For readers familiar with Freire and Smith, it's important to note that I'm not arguing that their approaches are identical or without contradiction. Indeed, Smith (whose writing takes up and extends the themes of institutional ethnography) would probably have scoffed at some of the existential formulations in Freire's writing. In particular, Freire's idea of an "ontological vocation" and the struggle to "become more fully human" (1996: 25) would likely have struck him as an unproductive detour into the snared terrain of ideological thought.

Nevertheless, there are significant points of convergence in Smith and Freire's approaches. This is particularly the case with respect to each writer's desire to break down distinctions between various forms of human activity. For Freire and Smith, education, research, learning, and struggle are actualized through the process by which they become inextricably bound to—and completed through—one another. Likewise, both Smith and Freire place significant emphasis on the role of confrontation in the process of knowledge production. Both insist, too, that learning must be based on forms of concrete investigation that begin from where people are located.

How can activists use these insights to help realize the potential of direct action in order to help us increase the effectiveness of our disruptions? To begin, it's useful to consider how confrontation can be both a tactical and an analytic procedure. As in Chapter 1, I emphasize how the moment of confrontation with the limits of representational action makes the possibility of a genuine politics—a politics based on production—possible. However, as will become clear, this process remained incomplete in the anti-globalization movement. Even at its point of greatest elaboration, it remained replete with contradictions in need of further clarification.

■

"Women must (appear to be) wearing a bra," read the ACC's account. Was the parenthetic qualifier part of the jail's policy? It seems unlikely. Instead, this sentence is probably best understood as an expression of a struggle between the rigid jailhouse code and the stern will and defiance of activism. More to the point, it represents a conflict between the letter of the law and the experience of existing within it, of trying to navigate its stipulations. Whether or not it actually happened this way, it's not difficult to imagine a member of the Anti-Capitalist Convergence going to the prison and being told that they could not visit their comrades on account of a transgression of one of these rules.

Perhaps the activist went further and challenged the prison official to provide an account of why these rules even existed. Through this process, she may have discovered that the overlapping and intersecting projects of incarceration and gender regulation were enshrined in a written policy. And, we might imagine, as the concrete practice of the jail became clearer, the mystifications through which it ordinarily gets perceived began to fade away. Although this interaction can only be inferred from ACC's disclosure of the policy for prison visits, the parenthetic note reveals something about a confrontation and an active moment of social research.

From the meticulous planning of logistics committees preparing large actions to the long hours individuals spend brushing up on the depravity of the bourgeois world, activists already engage in extensive amounts of investigation aimed at making their movements more effective. However, as of yet, there have been very few systematic attempts to use movement participants' experiences of confrontation as the starting point for research. There have been even fewer attempts to turn movement activists themselves into conscious, organized, and effective researchers. Such an attempt, I feel, would allow for a considerable escalation in both the level and effectiveness of our struggles.

Is activist research of this sort possible? A cursory glance suggests that the general orientation toward direct action within the anti-globalization movement spontaneously satisfied many of the criteria for effective social research outlined by George Smith. In his 1990 essay "Political Activist as Ethnographer," Smith suggested how, since we are located outside of but in constant interaction with "ruling regimes" (like the prison in which the Jane Does were held), activists could explore the social organization of power as it was revealed through moments of confrontation (1990: 641). In this way, confrontation becomes the basis not only for tactical innovations but for epistemological ones as well.

How, then, might this capacity for research be clarified and extended so that it is able to provide us with reliable knowledge that we can draw upon while making strategic and tactical decisions? This question becomes especially important when we consider how, even though the carnivalesque abundance of the movement played an important role as a life-affirming impulse, it remained insufficient as a basis upon which to extend disruptive capacities. However, by challenging the formal distinctions between research, education, and disruption, and by engaging in activism as producers (and not merely critics) of social relations, activists could considerably extend the possibilities of transformative intervention.

It's in light of this possibility that the confluence between the direct action ethos and Paulo Freire's conception of education as an act of freedom becomes especially clear. As a practice of resistance, but also as a method of engaging with the world that throws many of its mediations into relief, direct action provides activists with a strategy of moving beyond what Freire, following Alvaro Vieira Pinto, called "limit situations" (1996: 83). By impelling conditions that require actively uncovering how social relations are put together and by forcing ourselves to enter more fully into the concrete details of social relations, direct action facilitates the demystification of the world in a manner not unlike that advocated in Freire's pedagogy. Even a brief appraisal of activist attempts to visit the Jane Does reveals how this is the case.

The entire Jane Doe situation and the knowledge people gained from it was made possible through a systematic commitment to confrontation. This commitment, which lies at the heart of the direct action ethos, enabled activists to push against limit situations. In this instance, conflict and learning began with the ACC's call to action for the People's Strike. In the context of police fears about losing control of American cities since the Battle of Seattle, this call-out led police to organize a massive operation that culminated in the mobilization of hundreds of riot cops. Even before activists had hit the streets, confrontation played a key role in producing the situations that led them to discover the policies that organize visits to DC-area women's prisons, and much more besides.

As many activists learned the hard way, police and lawmakers during this period worked to expand the category of "confrontation" to such an extent that it encapsulated many apparently non-confrontational practices. In the context of anti-globalization protests, it was not difficult to wind up in custody. This was the case with the Jane Does. Picked up for failing to disperse when they were ordered to, the Jane Does—once arrested—continued their confrontation with police by refusing to comply with the institutional mechanisms through which they would be processed. Finally, by taking an active interest in what was happening to the Jane Does, ACC activists came into confrontation with the bureaucratic mechanisms regulating interactions between inmates and those who would visit them.

While this small piece of information might not initially seem to be especially important when considered in the overall context of the fight for global justice, it's critical to remember that this knowledge was gained during (and determined by) the course of struggle itself. And while, in this case, it appears to have happened accidentally, allowing the course of struggle to determine our research agenda is not a bad idea. Indeed, it was a central premise of Smith's political activist ethnography. Start where you're at. Map your way out. Watch the interconnections proliferate. Recounting his experience doing research to further gay liberation struggles and AIDS activism, Smith confides that he did not base his work on separate or formal interviews. Instead, "the route of access was determined by the course of confrontation, which in turn was determined ... by analyzing the data. Thus the research had a reflexive relation to the political struggle of people" (1990: 641). Dissidents in the anti-globalization movement were on the verge of making this discovery.

■

For the Jane Does, confrontation helped to reveal a small but significant piece of the social regulation puzzle by uncovering a connection between gender and the carceral project. What happens, then, if we try to make sense of this small discovery in the context of the anti-globalization movement as a whole? Although arrest is not the only place that confrontational research can lead, it is an important point of contact between dissidents and the conceptual relevancies of ruling regimes. And there have been plenty of arrests. During the People's Strike alone, more than 650 activists were arrested.

In Seattle, approximately 500 activists were picked up; nearly 500 more were arrested in Quebec City during demonstrations against the Summit of the Americas; more than 200 were nabbed in New York during protests against the World Economic Forum in February of 2002; hundreds more were booked in each of Genoa, Gothenburg, Prague, and other protest venues between 1999 and 2001. On top of this partial list, we must remember the A16 actions in Washington, DC, where it is estimated that nearly 1200 people were arrested in a week of protests against the IMF and World Bank.

All told, since the Battle of Seattle, several thousand anti-globalization activists were able to directly learn something about the state while spending time in its custody. And though the state seemingly relied on arrest during this period as a means of diverting activist energies and breaking organizing momentum, this regulatory strategy often led to a new fearlessness. The repressive apparatus of the state, once exposed through excessive use, ceased to generate the same trepidation that it did when its machinations were unknown. Again, we find traces of George Smith: "being interrogated by insiders to a ruling regime, such as a crown attorney," Smith pointed out, "allows a researcher to come into direct contact with the conceptual relevancies and organizing principles of those bodies" (1990: 640). And so it was that, in swallowing us, they exposed their squishy insides, their ineptitudes, and the causes of their indigestion. Through the concrete experience of arrest, many activists came to a better understanding of how the system actually works and managed, in a manner of speaking, to inoculate themselves against its mystifications.

However, while direct action can play an important role in the process of demystification, demystification itself remained—at best—a secondary consideration for many activists. A result of the habits and contradictions endemic to white and middle class experience, many activists approached these moments of confrontation from the standpoint of what these actions were thought to *mean*. And though they were engaged in confrontations that unearthed the social organization of the material world, many activists remained oriented to (and motivated by) *a priori* conceptions. George Smith observed a similar tendency amongst activists fighting against the policing of gay men and for treatment options for people living with AIDS. According to Smith:

> Rather than critiquing the ideological practice of ... politico-administrative re-
> gimes as a method of determining how things happen, activists usually opt for
> speculative accounts. The touchstone of these explanations was the attribution
> of agency to concepts... Instead of events being actively produced by people in
> concrete situations, they are said to be "caused" by ideas. (1990: 634)

Although ideas give shape to the conceptual relevancies that are made ac-
tionable in any course of events, events themselves are not caused by ideas but
rather by concerted and coordinated forms of social action and organization.
Significantly, ideas themselves find their condition of possibility in the same
arrangement. In other words, the cause of events (and even of ideas themselves)
cannot be found in ideas. It must be located instead in forms of organized and
coordinated social action. And while ideas, especially when they converge to
form an ethos of struggle, can be powerful motivating forces, they do not in and
of themselves cause those who are motivated by them to realize their objectives.
This requires a form of translation through which the ideal is forced to come
to terms with the material world. In other words, at the point of its opera-
tionalization, it ceases to be an "idea" and becomes instead a form of socially
coordinated action. In order to make our struggles more effective, it's therefore
necessary for dissidents to overcome the mystifications of idealist thought. And
dissidents are often more attentive to the dynamics of the world than most.
Nevertheless, we still succumb to our own forms of wishful thinking.

For Freire, abstract thought was a principal barrier to transformative engagement. This is because conceptual abstraction allows for the resolution of
social contradictions at the representational level while, at the same time, concealing the necessity of elaborating a politics rooted in production. "Closing
themselves into 'circles of certainty' from which they cannot escape," Freire
argues, people committed to conceptual abstraction "'make' their own truth."
But there are limits to solipsism:

> It is not a truth of men and women who struggle to build the future, running
> the risks invoked in this very construction. Nor is it the truth of men and
> women who fight side by side and learn together how to build the future—
> which is not something given to be received by people, but is rather some-
> thing to be created by them. (1996: 20–21)

Because these individuals transpose the world into the register of ideas
(because, in this way, they treat history in a "proprietary fashion"), they "end

up without the people—which is another way of being against them" (1996: 20–21). Pushed to its ultimate logical conclusion, Freire's insight suggests that movement unity and coherence is best achieved not through tactical moderation (as was often proposed) but through the inescapable truth of confrontational production.

∎

I first got a sense of this in 1997 during an occupation of the president's offices at the University of Guelph. Provoked by government plans to increase tuition, the occupation represented an attempt by students to address the growing inaccessibility of Ontario universities. Although the provincial Tory government had been systematically raising tuition since its election in 1995, by 1997 (perhaps in an effort to avoid criticism for its anti-education policies), it left the tuition increase to the "discretion" of individual universities. This localization of decision-making power allowed dissidents to begin reconsidering the manner in which they approached struggle.

Ontario students had been opposing attacks on education for years. However, the "discretionary" tuition increase fundamentally changed the dynamics of student activism. Before 1997, Ontario students would regularly gather on the lawn of the provincial legislature to raise their voices in moral outrage. Since the actual processes involved in implementing educational policy were opaque to most of us, all that was left to protest was a governing "anti-student" ethos. Assembled in front of the legislature, students would learn about "the issues" but could not intervene in the events shaping the future of education. In 1997, with the purported shift in decision-making power from the province to the university itself, many students were provoked into looking closely at our own institutions, perhaps for the first time. A whole world of specificity began to unfold.

Occupation impelled the need for a new kind of knowledge of the university and its social relations. In order to get into the president's offices in the first place, activists had to become familiar with mundane aspects of the building and its operation. A discernable shift in student politics took place. Once a measure of commitment and engagement, being "informed about the issues" was quickly surpassed by the need to develop an intricate knowledge of actual social relations. At organizing meetings leading up to the occupation, activists began compiling lists of things we would need to know in order to proceed: "When do the janitors unlock the door from the stairwell to the administrative floor?" "How many doors lead in and out of the space?" "Will we be able to lock them?" "Once inside, what will we do if administrators or office staff are already there? Is it better, legally speaking, to force them to leave the office before locking the doors or risk the possibility of locking them in and being charged with forcible confinement?"

A process of research and concrete investigation ensued. According to Smith, when investigating the "extra-local realm," it's necessary for "the local experiences of people" to "determine the relevancies of the research." This is because these experiences "point to the extra-local forms of organization in need of investigation" (1990: 638). Although none of us was versed in Smith's work at the time, it was in this manner that we proceeded. Starting from our initial point of local confrontation, we began looking outward and asking specific questions about the organizational processes that impacted upon the immediate situation.

These organizational processes were often enshrined in and made possible through texts. Both the Criminal Code of Canada and the University's Code of Student Rights and Responsibilities came into view as potentially significant. Since these texts weighed heavily on the local situation and gave it its social character, activists needed to consider how their activities would be interpreted and made intelligible. At the same time, however, activists also considered how the regulatory process of textual inscription might be dodged, subverted, or made irrelevant through decisive action. Continuing well after the action itself, this new approach to confrontation changed the way we understood the university and the world beyond its walls. Resulting from an epistemic shift demanded by the action itself, research, pedagogy, and production each became important (if under-articulated) aspects of our activist practice.

■

But students were not the only actors in the confrontation dynamic. Arriving to find locks and chains on their doors and barring the entrance to their offices, administrators began making urgent pleas, backed by threats, that the occupiers not read or tamper with files in the offices. Files, after all, are a critical part of the infrastructure that makes a ruling relation possible. Initially, the administration knew this more than the occupiers did. It was their domain, after all. However, through confrontation, the importance of the files was revealed to the activists as well. (In retrospect, we should have been much more curious—and more disruptive, too. The occupation only began to scratch the surface of what we didn't know about the university and how it worked.)

After assuring the occupiers that hell hath no fury like a bureaucrat whose files have been tampered with, the administration's next course of action was to call the city fire department. With the doors locked, the administration reasoned, the occupation was a fire hazard and posed a threat to the "safety of students." Although, in the end, the firefighters did not intervene, the incident revealed something important about how physical spaces are often regulated. Since then, I've noticed how common it is for authorities to cite fire code violations when evicting activists from squatted buildings or organizing centers. Zoning laws, fire codes, property titles: these are the texts that make it possible for ruling relations to be coordinated and enacted in actual spaces in the actual world. And because these texts prompt standardized and universal courses of action to address ideologically construed local "situations," they can be mobilized to regulate a multitude of moments that, from the standpoint of experience, can appear to be completely unrelated. Given the regulatory capacities they enable for those in power, these texts are thus of supreme importance to activists as well.

Although we were not fully aware of it at the time, the occupation provided us with a way to begin piecing together a concrete understanding of how the university worked. However, despite the intensity of our engagement, learning was not limited to those of us directly involved in locking down the site. By forcing the administration to act in ways to which it was unaccustomed, we were able to throw into relief some previously invisible dynamics. These became evident to everyone on campus. Consequently, there was a palpable shift in the character of discussions between students. Although it had not been our initial intention, the confrontation produced by the occupation created an important pedagogical moment.

■

With the rise of the anti-globalization movement, I began conducting workshops on direct action and street tactics. With an academic background in critical pedagogy and a desire to make struggles against globalization as effective as possible, I became very interested in the problem of designing a workshop that would prepare people to engage in sometimes frightening confrontations. Since many workshops I had attended took place immediately before major actions, they tended to focus on lists of things that activists "needed to know."

Don't wear contact lenses; don't lose your buddy; remember not to say more than required while under arrest; remove pepper spray with mineral oil followed immediately by rubbing alcohol: our lists were certainly notable for their esoteric contents. But despite this novelty, our direct action workshops never strayed too far pedagogically from the banking model of "education" critiqued by Freire. Activists were being equipped with lists of what to know; however the more difficult problem of *how* to know still needed to be addressed.

When I began conducting my own workshops, I noticed that participants often felt that they couldn't engage in any activities until I defined direct action. Although my workshop began with an exercise in which participants were asked to situate themselves in relation to whatever conception of direct action they currently held, for many, this was insufficient. Until I described what *I* meant by direct action, some participants intoned, there would be insufficient grounds for collective learning. The workshop participants' concerns highlighted two related problems. The first was that, despite the fact that everybody talked about it, there continued to be profound ambiguity about the meaning of direct action within the movement.

The second and more significant problem was that, despite being the epistemic premise of the very powers we were fighting, activists attending my workshops often expressed a strong desire to start from the standpoint of concepts and explain their experiences from there. While *knowing* is an act made possible by deliberate and productive engagement with the world, what activists at the workshop often sought was *knowledge*, the objectified residue of knowing. As workshop facilitator, I was expected to convey this knowledge, which was perceived as static, universally applicable, and transferable from situation to situation. The social specificities that prompt knowing—and the knowing of workshop participants themselves—were forgotten in the leap toward abstract thought.

For Dorothy Smith, this way of thinking is an important component of contemporary ruling regimes. In *The Conceptual Practices of Power*, she explains how, in a ruling relation, subjective experience is conceived in opposition to the objectively known. "The two are separated from each other by the social act that creates the externalized object of knowledge—the fact."

> Facts mediate relations not only between knower and known but among knowers and the object known in common... A fact is construed to be external to the particular subjectivity of the knowers. It is the same for everyone, external to anyone and ... is fixed, devoid of perspective, in the same relation

to anyone. It coordinates the activities of anyone who is positioned to read and has mastered the interpretive procedures it intends and relies on. (1990: 69)

Since I was the workshop facilitator, I was cast in the role of dispensing the facts, the knowledge particular to "the workshop"—a form of social organization with its own conventions and interpretive procedures. Under these conditions, it's not surprising that I was called upon to provide a definition of direct action. Such a definition, according to the standards of objectified knowledge, was a universal object that I could dispense; an object that anyone, provided they had come to my workshop, could receive. Needless to say, I found that this approach bore a strong and disconcerting resemblance to the "banking" model of pedagogy critiqued by Freire. In this model, knowledge is construed as an object that can be "deposited" into the student, the passive recipient. According to Freire, in the banking model, "the teacher talks about reality as though it were motionless, static, compartmentalized and predictable or else he expounds on a topic completely alien to the existential experience of the students."

His task is to "fill" the students with the contents of his narration—contents which are detached from reality, disconnected from the totality that engendered them and could give them significance. Words are emptied of their concreteness and become a hollow, alienated and alienating verbosity. (1996: 52)

I shuddered at the thought that this "teacher" could be me. Having spent the last several years of my life trapped in the academy, I knew that I was sometimes guilty of "alienating verbosity." But hadn't I been the one pushing workshop participants to generate an account of direct action derived from their own experiences? Had I not, further, encouraged participants to think about confrontation as a productive dynamic? Was it the workshop itself, with the interpretive structure that it demanded, that led participants to want to set a universal definition of direct action and empty it of its concreteness? I was perplexed by the disappearance of workshop participants as knowing subjects. What became of the subjects who could use experience as the starting point for developing an understanding of the social world so that they could better transform it? Did the workshop swallow them? Or was there something about our presuppositions concerning direct action itself that led us back into the world of conceptual abstraction and representational knowledge?

■

When participants at these workshops did refer to their experiences, it often took the form of testimony. They spoke in a way that seemed less about developing an understanding of the world by investigating concrete situations and more about telling a personal truth. While it was good to hear accounts of people's experiences, these did not bring us much closer to understanding social relations or determining how we might blow them up. Although they did not start from the standpoint of reified objective "knowledge," these testimonial accounts would often go to the opposite extreme and assert subjective experience *as* truth. Adopting the narrative voice that Freire identified as the defining tool of banking pedagogy (1996: 52), workshop participants would end by entering experience itself into the realm of objectified knowledge. Often, this would produce situations in which the presented knowledge-objects would stand in sharp contradiction with one another.

What could be done? Following the conventions of post-modern politeness, should we have concluded that the situation leant itself to multiple readings? This seemed depressing: we weren't talking about twentieth century working-class Irish novels, after all. We were talking about the social relations that made up the terrain upon which we struggled. Surely, there was something concrete that we could actually know. How could we find it? What seemed to be required (as George Smith succinctly outlined) was not a "shift from an objective to a subjective epistemology … but rather a move from an objective to a reflexive one where the sociologist [and the activist!], going beyond the seductions of solipsism, inhabits the world that she is investigating" (1990: 633).

Likewise, in *Pedagogy of the Oppressed*, Freire cautions about the shortcomings of both "objectivism" and "subjectivism." As with Smith, Freire suggests that what is needed is a form of praxis that breaks down the dichotomy between subject and object. Starting from within the realm of situated experience, this approach plays itself out on the world of objects through a process of broadening and socializing subjectivity. "The more people unveil this challenging reality which is to be the object of their transforming action," Freire argues, "the more critically they enter that reality" (1996: 35). By "entering that reality," which is the object of their activity, the subject ontologically *becomes* the social. In this way, conscious production (the transformation of the world of objects and social relations) becomes the means by which activist-researchers transform themselves.

For Freire, understanding this process first requires that the relationship between subject and object be properly understood. "To present this radical demand for the objective transformation of reality, to combat the subjectivist immobility which would divert the recognition of oppression into patient waiting for oppression to disappear by itself," he suggests, "is not to dismiss the role of subjectivity in the struggle to change structures."

> On the contrary, one cannot conceive of objectivity without subjectivity. Neither can exist without the other, nor can they be dichotomized. The separation of objectivity from subjectivity, the denial of the latter when analyzing reality or acting upon it, is objectivism. On the other hand, the denial of objectivity in analysis or action, resulting in a subjectivism which leads to solipsistic positions, denies action itself by denying objective reality. Neither objectivism nor subjectivism, nor yet psychologism is propounded here, but rather subjectivity and objectivity in constant dialectical relationship. (1996: 32)

Since I was beginning to suspect that direct action contained a strong revelatory impulse, I was frustrated that personal activist experiences were so regularly transposed into a narrative, story-telling frame. It seemed odd that direct action, which had been so pedagogically generative during the occupation at the University of Guelph, could be reduced in workshops to either testimonial utterances or lists of things to remember. Despite the potential of becoming an effective research practice and strategy for the conscious production of new social relations, and despite real similarities with Freire's pedagogy and Smith's activist ethnography, discussions about direct action in the workshop setting erred toward banking and not problem-posing pedagogy, toward abstract and not reflexive understandings of the social. Why was this so?

■

Although direct action compels activists to adopt a problem-posing approach that encourages confrontations with limit situations, activists have also demonstrated a continued reliance upon conceptual abstraction. This seems to be especially true when activists try to explain what direct action is. Although direct action has allowed activists to confront limit situations and break abstract and solipsistic "circles of certainty" (Freire 1996: 20), it has not always proven to be effective in breaking the binds of idealist abstraction or the facticity of ruling regimes. Rather than existing in dialectical interaction (as Freire and Smith both propose), practice seems here to be ahead of theory. It's a disjuncture that finds expression in the written accounts of activists themselves.

The following passage, drawn from the pages of the *Anarcho-Syndicalist Review*, is an excellent case in point. As a piece of writing, it's exceptionally bad; however, the frustration experienced in reading it is not the result of poor writing alone. Indeed, the solipsistic sentence structures appears to have less to do with literary deficiencies than with an abstract conceptual world spinning out of control. "From an anarchist perspective," the writer begins:

> Direct action is connected not only to solidarity, but also to what tends to be the precondition for solidarity and the underlying principle of the concept of direct democracy: non-hierarchical human communication. Such communication lies at the root of what direct action always is, individual and collective self-empowerment. As direct action contains its own end, within that self-defined end its meaning is also found. The more the ends are manifested in the means, the more it is direct action. (Beyer-Arnesen 2000: 11)

Conceptually, this is quite elaborate and complicated. And while it's true that not all movement accounts of direct action are this indecipherable, it's important to acknowledge that many activists have had difficulty providing a clear articulation of the term. This passage, then, can be read as a hyperbolic reflection of a more general problem. Given that this definition was published in a movement magazine's feature on the topic suggests that it's not merely the matter of one writer's anguish or incomprehensibility, nor the result of lax editorial protocols.

What's at work in this passage? First, by situating his account within an "anarchist perspective," the writer provides the interpretive procedure through which to read the rest of the account. Direct action becomes a knowledge-object. Second, the writer enters the world of predetermined logical concepts, drawn out in an interlocking constellation of abstract relations. Direct action is connected to solidarity. Solidarity and direct democracy are connected to and have their precondition in non-hierarchical human communication. Non-hierarchical human communication is, in turn, the definition of what direct action always is (individual and collective self empowerment, remember?). Snap! The circle of certainty closes.

Fortunately, not every attempt to define direct action comes to such unhappy ends. Nevertheless, as an approach to making sense of the social relations in which we engage, activists frequently begin from the perspective of the concept (self-empowerment, direct democracy, non-hierarchical human communication) and never entirely work their way out. Materials produced for distribution during the People's Strike by DC's Justice and Solidarity Collective show strong signs of this conceptual imbrication. The Collective, which functioned as a legal support team for activists during the protest, issued a leaflet instructing demonstrators on how to deal with cops showing up at their doors in the lead up to or during the action. Written in convenient point form, the leaflet provided the following instructions:

> Write down the names and badge numbers of all police officers

> Write down the names, job titles and departments of any fire marshals, building inspectors, or other government officials that enter with the police or independently

> Write down an inventory identifying everything being searched and/or confiscated, where in the center it comes from

The leaflet is standardized knowledge, a textual list of procedures that can be initiated by activists in multiple local settings. In order to accomplish this effect, the leaflet follows the conventions of writing adopted by ruling institutions. The effect of this form of writing is to turn specific experiences of encounters with police into a series of universal knowledge claims that can then be used to organize the practices of activists. Dorothy Smith has described how this kind of writing is achieved by transposing the experiences that produce knowing into universal, "textual time."

In this transposition, the active processes that led to the production of the textual account are rendered invisible. However, while the leaflet presents itself in a way that obscures the concrete experiences underlying its knowledge claims, it's important to note how, in this case, the transposition of activist knowledge into textual time is never fully completed. A trace of the concrete experiences that compelled the knowing upon which the text is based is left behind. Even as the Justice and Solidarity Collective provide universal procedures for activists, the everyday world cannot help but make a symptomatic appearance.

The leaflet presents general guidelines for coming through police visits as unscathed as possible. These guidelines are written in such a way as to be useful to activists in a variety of local circumstances. However, the Collective's suggestions—and what they anticipate as possible during a police visit—almost certainly emerge from the experience of anti-globalization actions where police have raided convergence centers using the pretence of fire code violations. Activists in DC were witness to such a raid during the A16 actions against the IMF and World Bank.

While the Justice and Solidarity Collective leaflet begins by talking generally about the "police" coming to "your home or workplace" (a framing which aims to cast its relevance as broadly as possible) by the end, the text has become much more specific. With the introduction of particulars that are neither "police" nor "your home," but rather "fire marshals," and "where in the [convergence] center" confiscated materials came from, the leaflet makes a return to specificity that betrays its attempt to speak in universal textual time.

Evident in the text, then, is a conflict between what people have learned through experience and the particular forms of textual production by which ruling regimes make the everyday world fall from view. Since these sense-making procedures divorce people from their own experiences, they stand at odds with the kind of concrete material reckoning that direct action makes possible. It's therefore not surprising to find that the Justice and Solidarity Collective's transposition of activist experience into textual time is only partially realized. What remains is a trace of the events that were then worked up into knowledge. As such, the leaflet can be read as a symptom of the split that many anti-globalization activists experienced between forms of concrete knowing arising from confrontation and forms of ideological thought.

For Dorothy Smith, it's precisely this split that provides a point of entry for investigating the organization of social relations. Especially for those who do not determine the content of representational abstractions but must live within them, the inevitable rupture between ideology and the everyday world signals the starting point for research. For Freire, the situation was nearly identical. Describing the contradiction of "progressive" educators using inherited pedagogical practices, Freire recounts how the ensuing discord can sometimes provide the oppressed with an opportunity to engage productively with the world: "Those who use the banking approach, knowingly or unknowingly (for there are innumerable well-intentioned bank-clerk teachers who do not realize that they are serving only to dehumanize), fail to perceive that the deposits themselves contain contradictions about reality."

> But, sooner or later, these contradictions may lead formerly passive students to turn against their domestication and the attempt to domesticate reality.

They may discover through existential experience that their present way of life is irreconcilable with their vocation to become more fully human. They may perceive through their relationship with reality that reality is really a process, undergoing constant transformation. If men and women are searchers and their ontological vocation is humanization, sooner or later they may perceive the contradiction in which banking education seeks to maintain them, and then engage themselves in the struggle for their liberation. (1996: 56)

However, while the contradiction between experience and deposited knowledge can function as an engine impelling people to act (an engine encouraging a more complete engagement with the social), this outcome is not guaranteed. It must be seized upon and elaborated within the framework of a conscious political production. For activists intent on learning from the experiences of the anti-globalization movement, the task is twofold. First, it involves developing a reliable knowledge of the social through productive and pedagogical confrontations. Second, it requires that what is learned through this process be transposed into an effective means of communication that does not abide by the epistemic conventions of our enemies.

■

Did the movement go far enough with its confrontations? Did we learn all that we could, or were the results as contradictory as the movement itself? A cursory investigation reveals that, even in the more militant sections of the movement, it was not always possible to push the process of learning from confrontation to its necessary conclusion. The "Communiqué on Tactics and Organization" penned by members of the Green Mountain Anarchist Collective (GMAC) in December of 2000 is an excellent case in point. While it was admittedly one of the more militant statements to come out of the movement, its conclusions seem profoundly incomplete.

"The following document is presented," they begin, "with the intention of furthering the basic effectiveness of our movement, by advocating various tactical practices that we hope will be adopted by the Black Bloc as a whole" (2000: 1). Throughout the communiqué, GMAC makes considerable efforts to outline how the concrete situation at demonstrations necessitates specific forms of organizing. They show how the Black Bloc could become more effective by developing a more formal and tactically reflexive command structure. In order to substantiate these recommendations, they produce a detailed account of police strategies used since Seattle. Recognizing the importance of maintaining control of the streets when trying to disrupt business as usual, GMAC exhorts discipline and organization. This is because, "at the present time, the mobilization of our forces is done in such a haphazard manner that our ability to combat well trained and disciplined State forces is limited" (2000: 7). In order to overcome this organizational and tactical deficit, GMAC proposed various command structures and disciplinary techniques aimed at extending activist control of the streets.

Making sense of GMAC's considerable emphasis on control of the streets requires that we acknowledge the tremendous energy that police forces devoted to addressing this same question. Before retreating to remote and inaccessible regions after the G8 demonstrations in Genoa, the anti-summit protest scenario had begun to take on the attributes of a medieval siege. Large perimeter walls were constructed to ward off demonstrators in Windsor, in Quebec City, and in Genoa. When this strategy proved to be too costly in terms of finances and legitimacy, global leaders made their way into the hinterland. During the 2002 meeting of the G8, delegates assembled at a remote mountain resort in Kananaskis, Alberta. In addition to strategies of geographic isolation and the erection of physical barriers, security agencies and private corporations also began investing considerable time and money developing "less than lethal" technologies aimed at controlling demonstrations.

Faced with these and other challenges, GMAC proposed several measures. They included: the formation of an elected tactical facilitation force; increased discipline and preparedness within individual affinity groups (including a division of labor between defensive and offensive forces, each outfitted with the appropriate equipment); extending reconnaissance and communications capacities; implementing a system of reserve forces that could be mobilized at a moment's notice; devising extra security precautions (including marking maps in code and using preplanned fluctuating radio frequencies for communication); circulating comprehensive communiqués after every action; engaging in physical fitness training between actions; and taking pre-emptive measures to diminish state capacities.

■

On this last point, "A Communiqué on Tactics and Organization" makes a very deliberate connection between the concrete situation and the forms of activity appropriate to addressing it. Drawing on movement experiences, the Collective writes: "The forces of the State are known to take pre-emptive measures against demonstrators prior to their actions." Given the previously mentioned raids on convergence centers, this can hardly be disputed. Furthermore, says GMAC, the police "regularly infiltrate us and make arrests before any general demonstration or acts of civil disobedience begin." Finally, the police also "start their tactical mobilization long before the sun comes up prior to the demonstrations on any particular day."

.   In order to neutralize this advantage, limited elements presently engaged in Black Bloc actions should independently take countermeasures. Here sabotage of police (and when necessary, National Guard) equipment is our best bet... If one of the primary advantages of the State is their mechanized mobility, then we should strike out against these repressive tools by effective, clandestine means. (2000: 20)

One is struck by the undeniably militaristic inflection of these proposals. While it is unquestionable that—if the goal is to beat the cops on the streets through tactical usurpation—the practice of sabotage would undoubtedly put activists at a greater advantage, the communiqué's analysis of the concrete situation nevertheless misses an important point. Who are the people who will do this sabotage? Where will they come from? The document is somewhat vague: "Such activities should be voluntarily coordinated by separate affinity groups under their own direction" (2000: 20). Roughly translated, this means: "someone else should do it." A contradiction thus arises. In order for the Bloc to be more effective, it needs to be more coordinated and disciplined. However, the intensification of coordination and discipline is made possible by (and requires, at its threshold) uncoordinated and clandestine actions. Such a limit situation would, of course, be fine if it weren't for the fact that the uncoordinated and clandestine actions were supposed to arise from within the ranks of the coordinated body itself.

So while the document challenges its reader to confront the idealism that would, for instance, eschew a "militaristic tone" (2000: 1), it nevertheless engages in its own form of wishful thinking. Specifically, it anticipates the possibility of turning the Black Bloc into a large, disciplined force capable of engaging in highly specialized and illegal operations against ruling regimes without looking at the broader dynamics of movement building. But these dynamics are also concrete social relations that must be explored and mapped. While GMAC correctly identifies many of the concrete measures that the state might take to make activists less effective (and does so in a way that obviously makes use of their own concrete experience), their analysis nevertheless fails to consider important aspects of movement building.

After all, the Black Bloc is not merely a clandestine organization. The question to be posed, then, is not how to use available forces to accomplish necessary goals on a plane where "us" and "them" are already constituted. Instead, we must ask how to change the balance of forces by reconstituting the plane itself. GMAC's contribution remains valuable because of its meticulous attention to the social organization of our opponents. What remains to be explained, however, are the specific conditions of an equally important and contradictory social force: the people.

The goal here is not to dismiss GMAC's contribution. However, because their analysis aims only in one direction (because it engages with questions of social organization without considering corresponding questions of pedagogy), it needs to be extended in at least one important respect. Specifically, we must broaden GMAC's insights to include considerations of movement building. These considerations must take into account both the not-yet-active and those who are active but have not yet acknowledged that they are, in fact, at war. In order for direct action to become a research practice and pedagogy, it must aim in two directions at once. In one direction we find our enemies: the state, the police, and the capitalist class. In the other, we find our friends, the people. But friendships must be cultivated. They are not always self-evident. And sometimes the things we do to build our friendships end up inadvertently undermining them. In the following chapter, I will consider some of these dynamics.

CHAPTER THREE

BRINGING THE WAR HOME

n the months following N30, activists began a process of assessing how their energies might best be directed. During this period, two interrelated concerns were prominent features of movement debates. The first concern—which was brought to the attention of many activists by Elizabeth Martinez's *Colorlines* article "Where Was the Color in Seattle?"—had to do with the overwhelmingly white composition of the movement. The second concern—formally articulated by Holland's EuroDusnie Collective in their article "What Moves Us"—had to do with the shortcomings of "summit hopping" as a strategy of resistance. For many white activists, the positive solution to these problems—especially in the period following September 11—took the form of a turn toward "local organizing."

However, activist accounts of their attempts to engage in local organizing during this period suggest that the move was fraught with theoretical and practical difficulties. In order to make sense of this impasse, I propose that—despite genuine and sincere efforts—activists were often thwarted by a conception of "the local" that was itself inadequate to the task they hoped to accomplish. This inadequacy manifested itself in two distinct ways. First, activists seduced by the promise of "the local" often failed to recognize how even their own white middle class "local" experiences could be a relevant resource to the project of devising strategies of social disruption. Second, since it was conceived as the abstract negation of summit hopping, the turn toward local organizing often sought positive content through engagement with "oppressed communities." Rarely was it recognized, however, that the concept of "community" often occluded the specific contradictions underlying the "local" settings with which activists sought to engage.

From these two distortions in the turn to "local organizing" ensued two surreal outcomes. Because they did not see it as an attribute of *their own* experience, many white activists found themselves in the unusual situation of having to *search* for "the local." Correspondingly, even though "the community"—conceived as the positive content of the abstract conception of "the local" championed by activists—could not help but express its contradictions, this did not prevent activists from elevating community members to the status of truth-teller.

For many activists, "the local" became an attribute of the Other and "the community" became a source of truth. Both of these outcomes proved harmful for movement development and both arose from a common incapacity. Owing much to the epistemic habits of whiteness, I argue that this incapacity is best understood as a still-incomplete break with ideological thought. Ultimately, it meant that anti-globalization activists were often unable to deal concretely with either the specificity of "the community" as a social formation or with the specificity and political relevancies of their own situated experiences.

As indicated in previous chapters, I do not take "ideological thought" to mean allegiance to any particular doctrine or belief. Rather, following Dorothy Smith, I use ideology to denote a series of social practices aimed at abstracting accounts of the world from lived experience and recasting them into universalized textual time (1990: 35–36). In this case, the concepts "local" and "community" serve as conceptual transpositions that end up concealing complex social relations. For activists intent on transforming the world, this kind of conceptual transposition of concrete social relations must be recognized as a demobilizing distortion.

■

The reasons that white middle class activists began to fetishize "the local" as a site of struggle can be gleaned from a consideration of the epistemic and ontological premises of whiteness itself. Drawing on Richard Dyer's assessment of the anxieties of disembodiment arising from white ontology and Rhadika Mohanram's account of Claude Levi-Strauss's telling distinction between *Bricoleur* and *Engineer*, I argue that white activists' love of "community" and their inability to conceive their own experiences as aspects of "the local" arise from an ideological reflex intrinsic to whiteness itself. Prompted by the anxiety of not really being present—an anxiety that, for Dyer, ultimately takes the form of a correspondence between whiteness and death (1997: 209)—white activists have sought out "the community" as a positive expression of "the local" and have infused it with valorizing and redemptive attributes. For white activists, "community" is the name of that place where people are thought to be really alive.

Readers familiar with the struggles of the 1960s will recognize how this situation bears a strong resemblance to the one recounted by Stokely Carmichael and Charles Hamilton in *Black Power*. In that text, Carmichael and Hamilton lament how many white radicals, "like some sort of Pepsi generation, have wanted to 'come alive' through black communities and black groups. They have wanted to be where the action is—and the action has been in those places. They have sought refuge among blacks from a sterile, meaningless, irrelevant life in middle-class America." (1967: 83)

Of course, whiteness was not the only factor at work in the movement's consideration of local organizing. Nevertheless, since the injunction to reorient toward communities emerged directly from critiques of the movement's whiteness, it's important to investigate the question on this basis. In this way, it's possible not only to call the habits of whiteness into question but to evaluate the strengths and weaknesses of the debate within the movement as well. What we are left with, for the most part, are white people, bereft of transcendental qualities, struggling to make sense of the world on the basis of grossly inadequate epistemic premises.

In what follows, I aim to provide an account of the debates around whiteness, "local organizing," and "the community" from the highpoint to the waning moments of anti-globalization struggles in Canada and the US. The course of the analysis starts at "the end" of the period in question with a brief overview of the 2003 European Social Forum.

■

Held in Paris between November 12 and 15, 2003, the second meeting of the European Social Forum was marked by a new sense of optimism. Those who attended the gathering, which took place just after the demonstrations against the WTO in Cancun earlier that fall, had every right to feel upbeat. Dubbed "the second Seattle" by many activists and commentators, the demonstrations were a remarkable affair. Confronted by massive opposition, the

WTO meeting wrapped up without accomplishing any significant business. Demonstrators blockaded roads, created eco-villages, squatted abandoned buildings, snake-marched through tourist districts and tore down portions of the eight-foot security fence surrounding the elite gathering. And while activists at the European Social Forum acknowledged that much work remained to be done, Cancun suggested that the setbacks that had befallen the movement since September 11 were surmountable.

Despite overwhelming odds, the movement had responded to the new political climate by deepening its analysis, honing its strategy, and reasserting in word and in deed that another world was possible ("We Are Building It!" trumpeted the title of one Social Forum workshop). As might be gleaned from sessions like "Thinking Globally, Acting Locally" and "Local Services in Front of Globalization," discussions at the Forum focused heavily on the question of how to make the movement a movement of the people, rooted in everyday lives and local settings. It is in this context that Hillary Wainwright, British activist and editor of *Red Pepper* magazine, led a seminar entitled "The Importance of the Local."

Throughout her speech, Wainwright took pains to emphasize the local dimensions of globalization. The privatization of public services, she argued, was but one example of the shift that had taken place as an effect of trade agreements and structural adjustment policies. Often, these shifts were made possible by (and helped to cause) cataclysmic disruptions of local settings. Consequently, the privatization of services had managed to provoke some of the most spectacular struggles against globalization. Often situated at the point of contestation, people in the global south were exemplary in their resistance.

For instance, in 1999, Bechtel was granted a forty-year lease over the Bolivian water supply. Almost immediately, rates for water jumped to around 25% of family incomes. By April of 2000, after the government was forced to declare martial law to quell protests, the contract with Bechtel was discontinued. Elsewhere, starting in 2001, the Soweto Electricity Crisis Committee (SECC) began to organize non-payment to Eskom, a state-owned electricity company in the preliminary stages of privatization. When the company cut people's electricity, SECC would reconnect it illegally, thus ensuring that people were able to continue running their homes. Gradually, the SECC campaign broadened to include defense of all basic services, including water.

Given these examples, it's easy to concur with Wainwright's assessment of the importance of local struggles. People *have* been effectively struggling around the privatization of services in the spaces they occupy—their neighborhoods, towns, and cities. And, given their success thus far, it's clear that these struggles are crucial to the project of resisting corporate globalization. Further, they suggest how the process of extending people's participation in all fields of life through attempts to socialize services might enable a corresponding extension of democracy.

Wainwright's comments were aimed at encouraging activists in the global north to learn from struggles over public services in the global south and to use them as models for their own actions in local settings. However, at the time of her presentation, many white activists were already working with a conception of "the local" that was very different from the one she proposed. Specifically, many seemed to champion a version of "the local" that had more to do with valorizing the experiences of people occupying particular social spaces than with investigating the situated expressions of trans-local processes. This "local" did not correspond to the place in which *the activist* was located; it didn't denote a particular point of engagement or a particular perspective. Instead, for many white activists, "the local" became a kind of code word for something like *the real site of struggle* or *where it's really happening*.

Prompted in part by early critiques of "summit hopping," anti-globalization activists in Canada and the US began advancing a conception of "local organizing" a full three years before Hillary Wainwright brought the issue to the European Social Forum. Discussions about the shortcomings of summit hopping were largely informed by a polemic written by Holland's EuroDusnie Collective. In their essay "What Moves Us"—released on the verge of the September 26, 2000 anti-IMF protests in Prague—EuroDusnie outlined the limitations of strategies centered on mass convergence. Under subheadings like "Summit Hopping is Only Possible for Western Activists" and "Summits are paired with Repressive Police Measures," the collective laid the foundation (and provided the language) for the debate.

Another important reference point in the turn from mass convergence to local organizing was Elizabeth Martinez's "Where Was the Color in Seattle?" (2000).[20] This often-cited text provided a framework for activists to connect the critique of anti-summit actions and the promise of "local organizing" to the question of movement participation by people of color. The argument was straightforward and hard to refute: if anti-summit actions were only possible for western activists and if they brought on repressive police measures, then it was little wonder that the movement had been (and continued to be) predominantly white despite the consequences that corporate globalization held for people of color. "In the vast acreage of published analysis about the splendid victory over the World Trade Organization last November 29–December 3," Martinez observed, "it is almost impossible to find anyone wondering why the 40–50,000 demonstrators were overwhelmingly Anglo." In her account, only about 5% of the participants in the action were people of color.

Although Martinez was not writing primarily for white activists, this did not prevent many from recognizing that her text had profound implications. Thinking about it now, many years after the fact, I can't help but be reminded of the profound satisfaction that many radicals took in citing indicting passages from Martinez's text in emails and movement documents. The purpose of these selections, it always seemed to me, was to use Martinez—as epistemically privileged voice of the oppressed—to settle the debate around exclusionary anarchist street tactics once and for all. In this way, and for those that recognized themselves as the target of the critique, "Where Was the Color" seemed to add fuel to the fire of white guilt. Such an outcome is, of course, hardly something for which Martinez must atone. However, the *reasons* white activists felt guilty need to be examined. For, while the record of historical injustice is not debatable, the same cannot be said for the means by which that past shall be redeemed.

■

Martinez built her story around a provocative passage in which a group of activists of color visit the Seattle convergence center and are forced into hasty retreat on account of the discomfort they feel. Brave enough to come to a predominantly white event at which they risked getting their heads bashed in by riot cops, the activists opt for the exit when they encounter a group of motley, foul-smelling white anarchists (who are, in Martinez's article, described in vivid olfactory detail). Martinez quotes one activist of color who described how, "when we walked in, the room was filled with young whites calling themselves anarchists. There was a pungent smell, many had not showered. We just couldn't relate to the scene so our whole group left right away."

The message is clear. These people could stand up to the state but they could not stand the odor, the scent of cultural exclusion wafting off these white bodies. To be sure, Martinez indicates that these activists eventually discovered they had a lot to learn from the anarchists. But this second insight never generated the same kind of engagement as the first one did. In the context of movement discussions, Martinez's comments seemed to corroborate the belief (held by many white activists) that the exclusion of people of color had to do with an ontological defect intrinsic to whiteness.

It's therefore hardly surprising that white activists began to act as though building links with communities "directly affected" by corporate globalization was a kind of redemptive practice—a transformative act of the first order. By the middle of 2001, discussions about "local organizing" provided a ready-made framework for this act of purification. Increasingly, "the local" became a synonym for "the oppressed community." Consider, for instance, this passage penned by activist Yutaka Dirks in the lead up to demonstrations against the 2002 G8 summit in Kananaskis, Alberta:

> This strategic shift (from summit hopping to local resistance) requires that we understand that struggle takes years of hard work building community based grassroots power, which is much different from the glory activism and frantic organizing which are prevalent in mass 'summit' actions. (Dirks 2002)

In addition to highlighting the need for "bold, creative and effective" tactics, Dirks argued that, "as numerous feminists and people of colour have stressed, [mobilizations] must also be part of a community based movement which is both sustainable and organizing to win." Correspondingly, "we need to recognize that struggles against poverty in our cities, struggles for self-determination by First Nations peoples, struggles against privatization and cutbacks across our country, struggles by communities of colour, and other struggles are all in resistance to capitalist led globalization." These struggles, which are counterposed to the frantic and ineffectual "glory activism" of "mass 'summit' actions," are conceived as inseparable from marginalized spaces and the people that occupy them.

Given the character of capitalist social relations in which trans-local processes are always actualized in local settings, activists are right to highlight local points of application. However, when struggles in local settings are undertaken without a concurrent investigation of the means by which ruling relations are trans-locally organized and enacted, then the community—rather than becoming the terrain of a broader struggle—is likely to degenerate into an emotive proxy. And activists have not always been good at tracing the trans-local relations. Writing in the wake of the anti-FTAA demonstrations in Miami, organizer Stephanie Guilloud pointed out that activists often privilege the moment of confrontation over the social context in which that confrontation takes place:

Even with all the time and privilege to pick and choose what issues we focus on, how many direct action activists from Seattle have tracked the direction of the WTO? How many know who the current director is, what their policies are, what effect these protests have truly had? Unfortunately, we rarely do the homework beyond the moment of engagement. (Guilloud 2003)

Following Guilloud, we might therefore ask whether activists who cannot find the threads of exploitative social relations in *their own* lives and *their own* localities (wherever these may be) can contribute anything meaningful to a discussion about confronting the trans-local process of globalization. But regardless of the depth of their engagement with the localities in which they found themselves, activists began to turn resolutely toward community organizing as early as 2000. Naomi Klein described this transition in the pithiest terms. "My e-mail inbox is cluttered with entreaties to come to what promises to be 'the next Seattle,'" she wrote.

It may be at the Republican and Democratic conventions in Philadelphia and Los Angeles this summer; or at the International Monetary Fund meeting in Prague in late September; or perhaps we shall have to wait until the Summit of the Americas in Quebec City in 2001. It is in the nature of this protest movement that we cannot predict when or how effectively it will strike. But is this really the way forward for protest—a movement of meeting-stalkers, following the trade bureaucrats as if they were the Grateful Dead? (Klein 2000)

Not content to leave the question rhetorical, Klein proposed that the movement had already begun a process of decentralization. By fostering horizontal affiliations across different communities in a manner that, to Klein, mirrored the rhizome-like proclivities of the Internet, activists had begun to prefigure the liberated society they wanted to create. "There is an emerging consensus," Klein suggested, "that building community-based decision-making power—whether through unions, neighbourhoods, farms, villages, anarchist collectives or aboriginal self-government—is essential to countering the might of multinational corporations" (2000).

Activists in Klein's account become the antithesis of the global: transparent where trade agreements obfuscate, direct where multinationals evade. Moreover, the movement "responds to corporate concentration with a maze of fragmentation; to globalisation with its own kind of localisation; to power consolidation with radical power dispersal." According to Klein, resistance was developing both new *strategies* and new *fields* of engagement. And the appropriate field for "community-based decision-making power" was, of course, the community.

■

By the time of the 2002 protests against the G8 meeting in Kananaskis, large numbers of activists had been fully converted to the paradigm of local resistance. And so, while some activists associated with the Toronto chapter of the Mobilization for Global Justice busied themselves filling a chartered plane to head out to Calgary (the nearest urban center to the summit site located in a remote mountain resort), others—associated primarily with Convergence des Luttes Anti-Capitalistes (CLAC)—began to organize a "regional action" for activists in and around Toronto, Ottawa, and Montreal. This action, which was scheduled to take place in Ottawa under the name "Take the Capital," was presented as marking a decisive strategic shift. In the callout for the action, the organizers made the terms of this shift clear:

> On June 26 & 27, 2002, the Group of Eight (G8) will retreat to the hills of Kananaskis for their annual Summit. In accordance with decisions made by the assembly at the Northeast Regional Consulta, which was held on February 16 & 17 in Ottawa, activists in the Northeast region have been organizing and mobilizing regionally and locally for "Take the Capital!," two days of resistance to the G8 in Ottawa on June 26 & 27. "Take the Capital!" actions will be undertaken in solidarity with demonstrations and actions against the G8 in Alberta and worldwide.

In both their callout and their promotional materials, "Take the Capital" organizers placed their commitment to local organizing in the foreground. And so, in addition to restating the PGA hallmarks under which they were operating,[21] the organizers emphasized "a focus on local organizing, as opposed to just going from one big protest to another" and "trying to make genuine links between 'anti-globalization' issues and local organizing efforts." However, while "local organizing" was stated as an important objective, the action itself was framed as a "regional mobilization."

This nomenclature is telling since it suggests a moment of transition between the "global" scale of anti-summit actions and the desire for "local" actions that were perceived as still being difficult to realize. The scale of the "regional" was envisioned as distinct from the "global" anti-summit protests that pulled people away from community-based issues. However, when the convergence took place, it closely followed the conventions of the anti-summit paradigm. With the exception of an important squat action that sought to address local housing issues, finding concrete means to struggle that did not draw from the anti-summit repertoire proved to be difficult. And, despite its "local" emphasis in the Ottawa context, it's important to remember that the establishment of squats was also a tactic used in Seattle. In the end, despite the fact that it was conceptually important, the distinction between "the global," "the regional," and "the local" seemed to disappear in practice. Why was this so?

■

As a term, "globalization" suggests the need for a macro-conceptual framework. Etymologically, "global" suggests that we're talking about the whole thing. However, as a socio-economic concept, "globalization" necessarily involves concrete practices in concrete locations. Globalization, like resistance, is something that people *do* in the world. Arjun Appadurai comes close to capturing the dynamic nature of this social process when he suggests that globalization "produces problems that manifest themselves in intensely local forms but have contexts that are anything but local" (Appadurai 2000: 6). The difficulty with this characterization, however, is that it suggests that there's some space where globalization happens that is *not* "the local."

The *context*, we are told, exists elsewhere. But where? If it exists in this world, then surely it is "local" to someone. And it's here that "globalization" (understood as a conceptual abstraction and not as a series of coordinated social relations) produces an equally abstract conception of "the local." The coherence of the conceptual distinction between "local" and "global" relies upon a familiar binarism that looks something like this:

GLOBAL	LOCAL
Macro	Micro
Universal	Particular
Masculine	Feminine
Economy	Culture
State	Community

This set of antipodal abstractions has appeared regularly in both activist discussions and scholarly debates. Practically, it meant that, while most anti-globalization activists in Canada and the US were convinced of the importance of local organizing by the end of 2000, the means by which to actually engage in local organizing against global capital remained opaque. Activist Jackie Esmonde succinctly summarized the problem: "demonstrating at the meetings of international power brokers has been exciting and important, yet the movement has not created the organizations or resources necessary for continued struggle."

> As a result, many now acknowledge that demonstrations at large international summits are insufficient and argue that the movement needs to create and build on the links between global political economy and local community... While the links between the global and the local may be fairly easy to understand in theory, it has proven much more difficult to put into practice. (2000: 2)

In hindsight, it appears that the difficulty we experienced when trying to move from "theory" to "practice" arose, in part, from the terms of the theory itself. "The global" (which, in Esmonde's account, is linked to "political economy") and "the local" (which is bound to "community") are each rendered as conceptual abstractions. It's therefore not surprising that they should only have a clear relationship to one another in theory. Like the macro and micro of sociological analysis, Esmonde's "global" and "local" may be useful devices for delimiting fields of investigation or accounting for the epistemic disjunction yielded by the unhappy marriage of objectivity and the partiality of embodied perspectives. What these terms do not provide, however, is a means of mapping the social. As a concept, "the local" is not yet a real place.

But activists like the ones that Esmonde was writing about were not alone in their struggles to make meaningful connections between local and global. It was a problem that found expression in academic publications as well. According to Carla Freeman, scholars who adopt the perspective of the global are likely to marshal radically different theoretical tools to those who concern themselves with the local. Because of this, the two scales—although conceptually interdependent—remain isolated. "Discourses on globalization have emerged within roughly two categories," Freeman reports, "those that emphasize global economics and those concerned with culture..." The resolution of this division has taken the form of "specific accounts of local contexts of incorporation into the global arena."

Scholars from a number of disciplines, including sociology, anthropology, and political science, have recently called for a greater focus on "the local" contexts of globalization as a way of bringing home the lived realities of these mammoth forces. (2001: 1008)

However, as Freeman points out, this new focus on "the local" has had the unintended effect of reiterating the theoretical alliance of the universal with the masculine and the particular with the feminine. "Localizing analyses of globalization," she maintains, "help to answer one set of problems while leaving another intact. This is evident where gender is concerned, for the turn to gender on local terrain has inadvertently been the slippery slope on which the equation between local and feminine gets reinscribed" (2001: 1009).

The solution, for Freeman, is to overcome the tendency to imagine the world as a composite of micro and macro moments and to trace the implications of broader social relations as they are made possible through concrete practices in actual locations. This means focusing on the local, not as a conceptual abstraction or an antithesis to the global, but rather as a concrete material setting made possible by social relations that are not immediately visible within its boundaries. Freeman explains:

> The assertion that we recast our view of contemporary processes we have labeled globalization through the study of the local cannot be a matter of subsuming one to the other, not a privileging of micro over macro, but rather a claim that understanding specific places, with their own particular and changing histories, economies, and cultures vis-à-vis the intensification of global movements (whether of trade, travel, commodities, styles, ideologies, capital, etc), helps us better grapple with the essence of these movements and their changing implications. (Freeman 2001: 1009)

Following this argument to its logical conclusion, we must acknowledge that, if pressed, it would be very difficult to say where we might find a space that is *not* "local" in the material sense. Even a meeting of the International Monetary Fund or the World Trade Organization (globalizing conceit of their handles notwithstanding) takes place in an actual and localizable place. How would the global/local distinction work here? Is the meeting "local" and the business conducted there "global?" If this is the case, how do we account for the fact that, in order for the "global" business to be worthy of the name, it must be actualized in local settings?

What becomes clear from this admittedly naïve line of questioning is that—since it requires the support of an abstract and antipodal conceptual constellation in order to become meaningful—advancing a universal category like "the global" actually becomes an *impediment* to grasping the whole picture. A concept, after all, cannot do the work of investigation. To suggest otherwise, Dorothy Smith explains, is to think ideologically. "The concept becomes a substitute for reality... What ought to be explained is treated as fact" (Smith 1990: 43).

Conceptual distinctions like that between the global and the local bring us no closer to understanding how globalization is put together through coordinated efforts in actual settings. The epistemic habits of whiteness confirm that rendering "the local" as an abstract antithesis to a universalized "global" makes it very difficult to acknowledge the materiality of local situations themselves. This is especially evident when these activists fail to see "the local" in their own neighborhoods, schools, or places of work. The implication, ontologically, is that white activists do not perceive themselves as living in "the local"—a position only made tenable by residual commitments to the white fantasy of disembodiment and transcendental subjectivity.

■

As critical geographers, anti-colonial theorists, and others have argued, this fantasy has been a central and enabling feature of Western bourgeois thought. However, while disembodiment gets presented as though it were a natural state of affairs, preserving the illusion requires a considerable amount of effort. Producing and maintaining the illusion of transcendental subjectivity has required, for instance, a particular and peculiar conception of space. In her writing on the importance of situated knowledge to feminist enquiry, Donna Haraway has described this conception as an effect of "scientific objectivity"— that "god trick" of being able to see everything from nowhere in particular (1991: 188).

But even with the god trick, it's difficult to argue that the Other doesn't exist in the same material world as the disembodied white knower. However, since the presence of the Other on the same plane tells the truth of the fantasy of disembodiment, white omniscience necessitates that another strategy be devised. Thus, in an effort to preserve the distinction, the *manner* of the Other's being in this world is made the site of difference. In *Black Body* (1999), Rhadika Mohanram identifies Claude Levi-Strauss's anthropological categories of *bricoleur* and *engineer* as expressions of this need to differentiate. As might be expected, the key ingredient is recognition of the Other *as* other.

Although, according to Mohanram, Levi-Strauss's anthropology makes efforts not to cast hierarchical valuations upon the epistemic differences he catalogues between the *bricoleur* and the *engineer*, this innocence is ultimately untenable. For the *bricoleur*, knowledge is thought to flow directly from encounters with objects and experiences of life in local settings. Levi-Strauss is fascinated, for instance, by the botanical knowledge of several African tribes, whom he imagines as bound to their habitat. For his part, although the *engineer* cannot match the *bricoleur*'s intuitive knowledge, he is able to corroborate and substantiate it through the use of universal scientific principles. The *engineer* is thus capable of producing meaning by forging connections out of abstractions. Here, meaning is a forced materialization, a form of organization *written onto* lived actuality.

Applying Levi-Strauss's categories to our current investigation, it's not surprising to discover that, while white activists (good engineers that they are) have had little difficulty imagining "the local" as a feature of the Other, they have encountered considerable frustration when trying to apply the concept to their own lives. As if by definition, the specificity of whiteness remains invisible. "The local," on the other hand, becomes the sign of embodiment, a beacon marking life bound by time and space. Edward Said noted a very similar dynamic in his study of *Orientalism*. How odd, he observed, that the whole scholarly specialization and geographical field of "Oriental studies" could be devised without an inverse. This is "fairly revealing," Said maintained, "since no one is likely to imagine a field symmetrical to it called Occidentalism" (1979: 50).

As has already been recounted, omniscient invisibility has been both a source of power and a source of anxiety for white people. On the one hand, occupying a position untouched by gross particularity has allowed white people to act on the basis of a transcendental conceit. For the white knower, the Other is thus cast as an object whose very existence is summed up by gross particularity. On the other hand, while omniscience has been a source of great power, it has also produced feelings of profound estrangement and disconnection from the world. It's therefore not surprising that many white activists have invested so much emotional energy in the search for some concrete referent. But rather than resolve the contradiction underlying white experience, this search for the concrete has tended to act instead as a kind of deferral. Recourse to the particularity of the Other becomes stabilizing ballast. Consequently, white people's "local organizing" in "the community" has often tended to reinforce rather than unsettle the delusion underwriting white experience.

■

In radical circles, "community" is often held up as a sacred term. Politically, it is thought to entail both a means and an end. Theologically, it approximates the collapsed continuity of the Alpha and the Omega. In this truncated eschatology, "community" is the sign marking both the reservoir of strength that enables people to struggle and the scintillating hope for which they struggle in the first place.

Like all concepts, "community" gains salience by referring to actual social relations. However, the transposition from social relation to conceptual abstraction means that the concrete specificity of the relation gets lost. Since both concept and abstraction—as the basic units of analytic thought—can never be done away with entirely, the task for those intent on changing the world is to devise concepts that do not curtail but rather provoke investigation. Instead of providing a means of transcendence into the realm of pure ideas, the concept should lead back to the world.

But rather than bringing us back to earth, the anti-globalization movement's concepts of "the local" and "community" tended to lead "out" of it instead. For the most part, white activists did not see themselves as living in the neighborhoods where "local organizing" was to take place. As a result, their conception of "the local" became intimately bound to a naturalized conception of community. In this iteration, "community" stood as both preserve and tribune of the oppressed. Consequently, many activists came to view the community not only as a specific point of application for neo-liberal policies, but also as a site of important insider's knowledge about the misery these policies generated. This knowledge, in turn, was often held to be the missing ingredient in an effective strategy of resistance.

In order to get a sense of this trajectory, it's useful to consider the work of the CrimethInc Ex-Workers Collective, a group that—although not universally loved[22]—nevertheless served as a powerful point of reference for disparate sentiments percolating in the anti-globalization scene. Taking aim at the dystrophic and sprawling suburban experiences of late capitalism, CrimethInc managed to give shape to (and amplify) a strong imaginative current in the movement.

It's therefore significant that, in *Evasion*, their compendium of hitchhiking, shoplifting, and slumming stories, the perceived connection between white middle class liberation and the ghetto is made explicit. Recounting the experience of a summer of train hopping adventures, an anonymous white and blond narrator recounts how, in East St. Louis, he comes into direct contact with the beauty of poverty.

> Small fires in abandoned lots, barred windows, and packs of kids pausing mid-hustle to watch the blond bum... I wondered if underclass solidarity would triumph over, you know, most white people actually *deserving* the force of blunt objects. I walked the residential blocks of East St. Louis for the charm of it all—people in the streets just kickin' it, bouncing balls and riding rusty ole bikes in the sun. I'd long understood "poverty" as synonymous with sunshine leisure on corroded implements of little or no resale value, with hurling yourself to the streets and *doing things*. (181)

Although the work published under the CrimethInc moniker is eclectic and heterogeneous, the passage cited above is not out of keeping with its general tenor. According to CrimethInc, modern existence (and, we might infer, for the white middle class especially) entails a substitution of survival for life.[23] From this premise, a logical consequence ensues: survival's ersatz arrangement can only be confronted by elevating *really living*—or "doing things"—into a political act of the first order. Practically speaking, this means trying to distinguish one's self from "most white people" (those that deserve the force of blunt objects) by cashing in on the promise of the messianic. As with Thoreau's *men* (who are like all other men with the exception that—for some reason—they elevate themselves by resisting the state), CrimethInc orients the reader to an internal compulsion that can only be understood in ontological-spiritual terms. Here's their account from *Days of War, Nights of Love*:

> Whatever medical science may profess, there is a difference between Life and survival... Their instruments measure blood pressure and temperature, but overlook joy, wonder, love, all the things that make life really matter... Many of us live as though everything has already been decided without us, as if living is not a creative activity but rather something that happens *to* us. That's not being alive, that's just surviving; being undead. (2000: 275)

Here CrimethInc make the connection between the deracinating experience of survival and Richard Dyer's white death anxiety explicit. It's therefore not surprising that, as a consequence of the visceral nature of their perceived connection to local experience, members of oppressed communities are often held to be teachers of the first order when it comes to the art of really living.

■

Although they remain its most earnest contemporary proponents, CrimethInc did not have to invent this perspective. During the late sixties, Martin Duberman recounted how New Left activists also frequently romanticized the people of the ghetto. Inhabited by the real salt of the earth, the ghettos were thought to be repositories of wisdom, honor, and virtue. Writing in *Partisan Review*, Duberman pointed out how many New Left activists often inadvertently reduced themselves to cheerleaders—good-hearted souls who rooted for the underdog while, at the same time, hoping that the underdog's effervescence would rub off on them. Because of this, the wisdom of the oppressed (seen as originating in the conditions of oppression themselves) came to be viewed, perversely, as a political *goal*. According to Duberman:

> It is this lumpenproletariat—long kept outside the "system" and thus uncorrupted by its values—who are looked to as the repository of virtue, an example of a better way. The New Left, even while demanding that the lot of the underclass be improved, implicitly venerates that lot; the desire to cure poverty cohabits with the wish to emulate it. (2002: 181–182)

In our own time, the habit of venerating the poor led many anti-globalization activists—and especially those seduced by CrimethInc's romanticism—to a life of slumming. These dynamics deserve careful consideration. However, it's important to remember that white activists have not been alone in mythologizing the community. According to several anti-racist feminist scholars and activists, the mythologized community has been a site of personal enrichment for men of color as well. In *Black Macho and the Myth of the Superwoman*, Michele Wallace traced how Black women's oppression actually *increased* under the heightened community sensibility of Black Power Harlem during the late 1960s and early 1970s.

When it was first released, Wallace's book drew extensive criticism from both Black radicals and white liberals who busied themselves flexing their newfound cultural sensitivity. These critiques compelled Wallace to write a new introduction upon reissue of the text in 1990. In that Introduction, she adopts a conciliatory tone and significantly qualifies many of the claims that caused controversy two decades earlier. Nevertheless, *Black Macho* remains an exceptionally lucid and scathing analysis of the uses to which "community" has been put. For Wallace, since Black Power struggles were effectively diverted (by shrewd white power brokers) into a bid for recognition of the value of Black masculinity, patriarchal control of the community and its women became a substitute for a more complete—and more costly—vision of liberation. Under these conditions, the amount of violence against Black women increased. According to Wallace, "the black woman pays an enormous price to walk the streets of her community."

> Only after she is sixty and weighs two hundred pounds is she given any peace. And even then at night she may be beaten up and have her pocketbook stolen. It is impossible for her to protect her children... Any black woman who's got any sense treads lightly in Harlem. (1990: 120)

Wallace's testament is a curt rejoinder to the New Left veneration of poor communities recounted by Duberman. Here, rather than constituting the self-evident ground of liberation struggles, "community" reveals itself to be a compensatory distraction and a dangerous site of gender oppression. But despite the obvious tensions between Wallace and the New Left, it's important to note how, in both accounts, "the community" is conceived as a natural category—as something that goes without saying. However, as Wallace's own account makes clear, there is in fact very little about what happens in the name of community that's self-evident or natural. For this reason, it's necessary to concede that—as a manifestation of ideological thought—the explicative category itself needs explaining.

■

This is difficult to do. Himani Bannerji has suggested that, within the social sciences, it has become increasingly common to treat "community" as an almost instinctive form of cultural association. On this basis, and in the context of contemporary social relations, it has become possible for "community" to assume the status of an effective category of ruling (2000: 160). Following David Harvey, Miranda Joseph has similarly argued that "'traditions of community' based on cultural and lifestyle distinctions, neighborhoods, or ethnicities have been invented ... to counter the antagonisms of class and to consume the overproduction induced by cycles of capitalism" (Joseph 2002: 28–29). Joseph extends Harvey's argument by proposing that "community" has not only been invoked to organize populations and redirect class conflict but also to foster a degree of auto-regulation at the level of the individual (29).

While Joseph acknowledges that "community"—because of its implication in the language of rights—might also provide grounds for resistance to capital, this possibility is marked by what she considers to be a profound ambivalence. For this reason, under contemporary conditions, it remains critical that those interested in a concrete conception of local organizing view "community" first and foremost as an ideological category so that they might, as Bannerji suggests, "develop a critique of the social organization, social relations, and moral regulations which go into the making of it" (2000: 154).

As with Wallace, Bannerji argues that making "community" the center of anti-racist struggles has been a dangerously ambivalent endeavor. In her estimation, uncritical support for communities of color has made it *more* difficult to highlight the forms of oppression that take place within them. For, while communities have a tendency to present themselves (at least, as Bannerji points out, in their representational endeavors) as homogenous bodies, they are in fact an amalgam of different and competing interests.

For Bannerji, the clearest of these differences are those between men and women. Activist expectations that "the community" can tell the truth of its experience under neo-liberalism tend to overlook or to ignore these differences. In the end, this often means that activists looking to oppressed communities for political direction (or, worse, political legitimacy) end up privileging the perspective of community patriarchs. In the period immediately after September 11, this dynamic became explicit as anti-war organizers fell over themselves to get Muslim clerics to speak at their rallies.

■

Thus far I've argued that—whether to learn how practices of oppression are put together across localities through coordinated social relations, or in order to throw a wrench in the gears of some smoothly functioning institution of privilege—resistance at the local level by whites is a minimum requirement for developing meaningful solidarity with those communities "most affected" by globalization. Instead of descending upon the sites of visible oppression in order to "help" the Other, white activists must learn to take responsibility for "the local" in which they find themselves and uncover the possibilities of resistance contained therein.

In light of this vision of trans-local solidarity, it's worth considering the Claustrophobia Collective, a group of US-based activists with affiliations to the Black Bloc and Anti-Racist Action. I first learned of this group when I was forwarded an interesting document that outlined how white activists from the anti-globalization milieu could offer meaningful support to Black communities in the event of civil unrest and riots. This document, entitled "Some Lessons from the Cincinnati Riots," circulated over the Internet for a brief period in 2001 and has been reproduced by several activist groups as a zine but has not, to my knowledge, been seriously examined or responded to in either the movement or scholarly press. Nevertheless, the Claustrophobia Collective's approach offers useful insights to white activists interested in developing a meaningful conception of local organizing. It's one that stands in sharp contrast to the stance of paternalistic empathy made tenable by fantasies of disembodiment.

The setting is Cincinnati in the spring of 2001. Police shoot a young Black man who had been guilty of committing a traffic offense. A group of people, both Black and white, descend upon a meeting of City Hall to demand answers. While in the meeting (at which they've been disruptive and noisy), they discover that riot cops have surrounded the building. After a brief standoff, the city quickly erupts into riot. Despite attempts by media and many politicians to identify the event as a "race riot," the Claustrophobia Collective's take is that the sentiment on the street was initially characterized primarily by anger toward the police. Nevertheless, many of the participants in the rioting are from the poor and Black neighborhood of Over-the-Rhine, a community that had become saturated with police as a result of "broken window" style enforcement protocols.

The Claustrophobia Collective put forward their "Lessons" in order to figure out how white activists and participants in Black Bloc tactics could contribute to riots like the ones that erupted in Cincinnati. What's striking about the document is the way that it deals with the questions of community, situated knowledge, and multi-racial organizing efforts. Written from "outside" the action, the document's writers nevertheless advance a meaningful and critical analysis starting from located experiences. In short, they neither succumb to, nor take direction from, the official "community" line. As they put it:

> What we're trying to do here is bring together and contribute our thoughts to discussions that have been happening among our networks—predominantly

white radicals organized around working-class centered anti-racist politics—about the possibilities for offering meaningful solidarity and support in a riot situation. Maybe the next time the black community throws up mass protests like this, we'll have thought things through and be in a position to support things better.

For the Claustrophobia Collective, "supporting things better" did not mean simply taking direction from the leadership of the Black community (who, in this case, threw their energies into a reconciliation and peace effort). Instead, it meant recognizing that riots are opportunities. The police can use them to escalate crackdowns in over-policed areas. Liberals can use them to gain political points. And activists can use them to build meaningful alliances in working class neighborhoods by extending solidarity and practical support. But what could white activists organized into anti-racist collectives contribute to a situation like the one that arose in Cincinnati? For the Claustrophobia Collective, the answer is as follows:

> Now all along we've been thinking of our role as white anarchists as trying to bring together two radical cultures of protest, to bring the strength of the 'black bloc' and radical direct action contingents that have successfully fought riot police at anti-capitalist demonstrations over the past few years to support the much quicker and more intense street fighting that flares up against police in the ghetto.

In other words, by drawing on their own situated experiences of struggle on the militarized streets of cities hosting elite summits, white radicals might make meaningful contributions to organizing efforts in communities of color. This is because each location is coordinated through a common trans-locally organized ruling institution: the police. And while there are clearly differences in the strategies deployed by police at anti-summit riots and in Black neighborhoods under "normal" circumstances, these strategies come more clearly into alignment when Blacks riot. Things level out at the top—especially when the cops feel constrained (as they do for the most part, and for the time being) to the use of "less than lethal" measures. In *Riots, Revolts and Insurrections* (1967), Raymond Momboisse—member of the United States' Riot Advisory Committee commissioned to write a report on urban insurrections after the Watts rebellion of 1964—points out how policing strategies follow procedures of escalation. The tactics used at peaceful demonstrations (or, alternatively, to keep a community in line) are designed to quickly make way for the tactics suitable to urban insurrections.

In "Lessons," the Claustrophobia Collective acknowledges that different experiences will yield different kinds of practical knowledge. However, this kind of practical knowledge is not confused with a fixed perspective or an ontological predisposition. Most importantly, different forms of practical knowledge emerging from different experiences are not viewed as being in competition. As partial perspectives, such accounts are instead viewed as a kind of experientially grounded objectivity.

As feminist theorist Donna Haraway has pointed out, objectivity *is* location. It's therefore possible for people in different locations to create a reliable map of the social using the same evidentiary standards. "The issue in politically engaged attacks on various empiricisms, reductionisms, or other versions of scientific authority," Haraway points out, "should not be relativism but location" (Haraway 1991: 194). If this is the case, and if the Claustrophobia Collective is right in their assessment, then it's inadequate for white organizations intent on offering solidarity to rioting Blacks to uncritically defer to their standpoint. Apart from amounting to a mystification of the conditions required for the production of reliable knowledge, such an approach also entails an abdication of responsibility.

■

At its worst, this abdication limits the kinds of resources that can be turned over to the cause of insurrection. Many white activists seem to fear that—if they articulate their perspectives in an upfront fashion—they will end up sounding like the know-it-all who caused so much hostility between white and Black activists in the first place. We might ask, however, what kind of solidarity can be achieved if white activists hold back and fail to contribute all that they know, if they defer to positions even when they ought to be criticizing them. In "Lessons," the Claustrophobia Collective takes up some of these questions.

> The Cincinnati Radical Action Group (CRAG), taking the line that the 'black community' had made its wishes known that radical whites should protest in white neighborhoods, called for a civil disobedience in Mt. Adams, an upper-class restaurant and artist district north of Over-the-Rhine. 80 demonstrators walked into the neighborhood and briefly blocked the streets

before police herded them onto the sidewalk, arresting and pepper-spraying 12 people... While the people who took part deserve respect for boldness, we had some problems politically with this action. It's hard to claim to take leadership from the 'black community' when there's no one viewpoint predominant in that community. And symbolically 'confronting privileged space,' while always fine, is not necessarily the same as supporting the struggle of the Black community. The demand that curfews should be implemented equally in rich white neighborhoods when they're imposed in the ghetto, while it's an appealing idea in its utter absurdity, is at the same time kinda irrelevant to the situation happening in Over-the-Rhine.

Evident in the Claustrophobia Collective's approach, then, is a clear break with the commonsense perspective adopted by many participants in anti-globalization struggles. This approach shares a strong bond with the principles outlined by Paulo Freire in *Pedagogy of the City*. In that book, Freire takes up some of the criticisms that had been leveled against his work since the initial publication of *Pedagogy of the Oppressed*. On the one hand, some accused Freire's pedagogy of pandering to the uneducated, valorizing them and claiming them as a fountain of spontaneous knowledge. On the other hand, some argued that Freire's pedagogy simply placed a nicer educator in the people's midst. The project of domestication, now less visible under cover of smiles, nevertheless continued to operate. Producing a synthetic argument that cut against both of these criticisms, Freire suggested that "to be with the community, to work with the community, does not necessitate the construction of the community as the proprietor of truth and virtue." Instead,

> To be and work with the community means to respect its members, learn from them so one can teach them as well...The mistake with the sectarian community-based program does not lie with the valorization of the people of the community, but in making them the only repositories of truth and virtue. The mistake does not lie in the criticism, negation, or rejection of academic intellectuals who are arrogant theorists, but in rejecting theory itself, the need for rigor and intellectual seriousness. (1993: 130–132)

In order to "be with the community," white activists who went through the experience of anti-globalization struggle and the subsequent turn to local organizing need to take our own location—in all of its boring specificity—more seriously. In order to do this, we must break with conceptual abstraction and discover grounds for local organizing that disavow the paternalistic valorization of the oppressed and foster the development of concrete solidarity. One basis for such solidarity can be found in the assumption of responsibility for one's own situated knowledge. Only from this perspective does it become possible to cut against the fantasies of disembodied white subjectivity, political omniscience, and the fetishistic elevation of those considered uniquely bound by gross particularity. In the following chapter, I consider the implications of this line of reasoning when applied to questions of gender.

CHAPTER FOUR

YOU CAN'T DO GENDER IN A RIOT

E arly in December of 2000, members of the ACME Collective issued a communiqué to the nascent anti-globalization movement. With the Battle of Seattle—and the Black Bloc actions that took place there—still fresh in people's minds, ACME's dispatch became a lightning rod for discussions about strategy and tactics. Marking the first public effort on the part of an anti-globalization-era US Black Bloc contingent to address the movement as a whole, the communiqué spoke primarily to a series of popular misconceptions about riotous actions. By compiling and then responding to "10 Myths About the Black Bloc," ACME helped to frame a discussion about the merits of property destruction at demonstrations in the cosmopolitan centers of the global north.

In addition to addressing their critics' concerns that the Black Bloc had not participated in planning the anti-WTO actions and that they had little grasp of the issues, ACME pointed out that many of their detractors believed that the Seattle rioters had simply been "a bunch of angry adolescent boys" and, hence, that their actions were inadmissible within the realm of serious politics. In repudiating this perspective, ACME pointed to its analytic superficiality. "Aside from the fact that it belies a disturbing ageism and sexism," said ACME of the adolescent boys theory, "it is false."

> Property destruction is not merely macho rabble-rousing or testosterone-ridden angst release. Nor is it displaced and reactionary anger. It is

strategically and specifically targeted direct action against corporate interests. (2001: 117)

With the tempest out of the teapot, anti-globalization activists began trying to make sense of the new political terrain. During this period, the Black Bloc (which, in Canada and the US, had been virtually unknown prior to Seattle)[24] quickly became an important site of gender struggle. Seeming to collect many of the most pressing contradictions of gendered experience and expressing them in one explosive moment, the Black Bloc forced activists to contemplate the gender of the riot. Initially, these discussions drew upon well-established debates about the problem of representation. Did the Black Bloc exclude women, as many activists held to be the case, or did it include them as some others had proposed?[25] Should women join in Bloc actions to make them more representative of the gender diversity of the movement, or should they condemn them as a persistent site of exclusion?

For activists in the movement, these questions—and the terms in which they'd been articulated—could not be avoided. Criticisms of the movement's perceived maleness resonated strongly with activists who sought to prevent their struggles from replicating the worst elements of the system they opposed. But despite almost endless discussions about the problem of exclusion, activists came to little agreement about what the solution—the ever-elusive inclusion—would actually look like. Could inclusion be achieved by opening up existing spaces and practices, or did it require changes in the practices themselves? Could women's participation be solicited, or were such efforts bound to be coercive and tokenistic? Despite the ambiguity of this new political terrain, for many activists one thing was certain: Black Bloc rioting and the politics of inclusion mixed about as well as petrol bombs and calming ponds.

In his position paper responding to the ACME communiqué, Brian Dominick pointed out that—despite the fact that ACME felt their actions resonated more with oppressed people than did the theatrical tactics adopted by other demonstrators—"the vast majority of oppressed people in this country didn't have the privilege to be in Seattle for this demo, even if they wanted to, and typically don't have the privilege of risking arrest at all."[26] In order to emphasize his point, Dominick concluded by remarking how "one is pretty privileged if one chooses to risk arrest in the way black bloc participants did" (2000).

As Dominick's position makes clear, the exclusion of marginalized people from political protest strikes most activists as unacceptable.[27] Consequently, if the paradigm of struggle works to exclude people of color, women, and other oppressed groups (as Black Bloc actions were thought to do), it becomes necessary to change the means by which struggle is conducted. This perspective quickly became commonsensical in certain movement circles.

I take issue with this commonsense on three grounds. First of all, the argument is based on the belief that women do not riot. History, however, does not bear this out. Second, the call to inclusion has tended to reify "woman" as a conceptual abstraction and has reinforced a representational logic at odds with genuine political transformation. This problem derives from mainstream conceptions (where the category "woman" still continues to enjoy relative stability) but also from tendencies within feminism that hold "representation" to be the principal field of political engagement. Finally, and perhaps most significantly, the movement's ongoing allegiance to "representation" (and its operational correlate, "inclusion") has tended to occlude the opportunities for gender abolition signaled by the anti-globalization riot.

■

Looking for representations of women in the history of rioting can be a disorienting affair. With the exception of a few early twentieth century sketches by German expressionist Kathe Kollwitz that depict women leading large crowds of starving peasants, women have tended to be represented in the European oil painting tradition and its derivative genres —if at all—either as the victims or muses of political action.

Figure 6: Kathe Kollwitz, "Outbreak" (1903)

Among the tradition's muses, perhaps the most famous is Eugène Delacroix's heroine in *La liberté guidant le peuple*. Depicting the ousting of Bourbons from Paris in 1830, Delacroix's painting places a woman at the center of the conflict. Liberté draws the mob into battle and, if we follow the narrative conventions of the genre, seems to assure their victory by her very presence. The work establishes a strong dramatic tension between *eros* and *thanatos*—a symbiotic but fraught interaction between the life-giving spirit of Woman and the capacity for men to bring death. The muse, as representational

Figure 7: Eugène Delacroix, "Liberté guidant le peuple" (1846)

ambassador of the transcendental Idea, has always been on hand to soften harsh realities. Nevertheless, this slaughter (like every other) was not achieved by the muse but by "the people"—who in this depiction are, in fact, a cross-class alliance of men.

So while Liberté might be the purported reason that these Parisians were compelled to fight (and men have long deluded themselves into believing that they fight *for* Woman), the fight itself does not taint her. In an otherwise dark composition, and for no other reason but to highlight her goodness, Delacroix's muse is enveloped in a light that seems to emanate from her very being.[28] Surrounded by armed Parisians, Liberté seems to float over the bodies of the fallen. Carrying the French flag, she is bound to the new republic even as she conceals the force that made it possible. Nowadays, Delacroix's image is more likely encountered as kitsch than as a serious political statement. And few will be surprised to find an image from the European oil painting tradition drawing on questionable metaphors and gender stereotypes. Nevertheless, by placing Liberté at the front of the insurrection "leading the people," Delacroix's image discloses an important debt to historical reality. And it is precisely for this reason that—even though she refuses both the muse and the transcendental feminine—Kollwitz has the woman in "Outbreak" occupying a similar place within the field of action.

Representations, no matter how distorting in their transcendental conceits, must nevertheless "represent" *something*. It's therefore not surprising to discover that, when one ventures beyond the frame of the art world, the historical record admits an impressive number of women—some well known, others lurking in the darkened corners of the archive—who have engaged in political violence. In *Labour in Irish History*, James Connolly (1987) rummages through the shadows to remind us how riots were often carried out in the name of women leaders. Describing the activities of Irish peasants in the middle of the eighteenth century during the establishment of British enclosures, Connolly recounts how "there sprang up throughout Ireland numbers of secret societies in which the dispossessed people strove by lawless acts and violent methods to restrain the greed of their masters, and to enforce their own right to life."

> They met in large bodies, generally at midnight, and proceeded to tear down enclosures; to hough cattle; to dig up and so render useless the pasture lands; to burn the houses of shepherds; and in short, to terrorise their social rulers into abandoning the policy of grazing in favour of tillage, and to give more employment to the labourers and more security to the cottier. (42)

Connolly mentions that the secret organizations conducting these acts of terror were very diffuse and often disappeared as quickly as they appeared. He does, however, draw special attention to the Whiteboys, a group that sought vengeance and justice in the South of Ireland. Wearing white shirts over their clothes in order to create an ominous uniform appearance while causing havoc at night, the Whiteboys are intriguing from our current vantage for their anticipation of the sartorial strategies favored by the Black Bloc. Connolly's interest, however, was piqued for different reasons. "About the year 1762," he mentions, "[the Whiteboys] posted their notices on conspicuous places in the country districts… threatening vengeance against such persons as had incurred their displeasure as graziers, evicting landlords, etc. These proclamations were signed by an imaginary female, sometimes called 'Sive Oultagh', sometimes 'Queen Sive and her subjects'" (42).

Although women are representationally absent from Connolly's history,[29] they are nevertheless conceptually present as imaginary leaders. The rioting Whiteboys were *subject to* Queen Sive, who might therefore be cast as an older sister to Liberté. But what sort of concrete situation might have allowed figures such as these to emerge? We can find hints in the riots themselves. Enclosure meant the separation of families from the land. Historically burdened with the responsibilities of home and family, the women of Ireland's pre-capitalist peasantry can truly be understood as motive forces behind the enclosure riots. It is therefore not surprising that the tumult should have been carried out in their name. For his part, Connolly presumed that Queen Sive—like her younger brothers Captain Swing and General Ludd—was imaginary. Though the riots may have been conducted *for* and *at the behest of* Ireland's women, it did not follow that it was therefore women *themselves* who conducted them. But whether or not there was an actual Queen Sive, historians since Connolly—Sheila Rowbotham notable among them—have affirmed that there were certainly women who rioted.

■

From the eighteenth century onward, there is an observable trend in women's participation in riots and other forms of political violence. Despite being representationally absent in many historical accounts, Rowbotham (1974) has noted that women were present in large numbers during historically celebrated moments like the storming of the Bastille.[30] Similarly, women were arrested in large numbers when the barricades of the Paris Commune finally fell. Many of them—women like Louise Michel, but also innumerable unknown ones as well—were subsequently exiled or executed.

Describing the early nineteenth century political scene in *Women, Resistance & Revolution*, Sheila Rowbotham (1974) recounts how women often participated in riots in a manner that reaffirmed their status *as women*. Since the majority of riots in England during the proto-capitalist period were compelled by what Rowbotham calls "consumption issues," they were intimately bound to the daily concerns of peasant women's lives. Torn between an earlier peasant experience and the dynamics of the new conditions, rioters often sought basic necessities. Very often, they would be thrown into action by fluctuations in the price of bread. Describing the tumult of one event in Nottingham in the year 1812, Rowbotham recounts how "mobs set to work in every part of the town."

> One group carried a woman in a chair who gave the word of command and was given the name of "Lady Ludd." Such actions were half ritual, half political. They came naturally from the role of women in the family. Their organization was based on the immediate community. They did not require a conscious long-term commitment like joining a union or party, nor were they feminist in any explicit sense. (103)

According to Rowbotham, even though these women were resisting the tyranny of their rulers, they were not yet challenging the system or their role within it. Often, peace could be reestablished through the market. With the price of bread set once again at the level determined by custom, things would often return to normal. "However," Rowbotham points out, "during the nineteenth century the context of the food riot changed because of the development of other forms of political action." Eventually, "the traditional action of women in relation to consumption became intertwined not only with revolutionary events and ideas but also with the emerging popular feminism of the streets and clubs" (103). In this way, the riot helped to inaugurate new forms of political subjectivity for women. Addressing immediate needs through violence translated, over time, into the capacity to *be* political and to begin envisioning a future beyond the family-consumption horizon.

■

By the beginning of the twentieth century, the violence of the British suffragette movement effectively transcended the logic of the consumption issue riot. Although suffragettes drew upon the spontaneous feminism of prior moments, the struggle for suffrage saw women riot not so much to preserve that which they required (or to which they felt entitled by custom) but rather to transform themselves into new beings. Through riotous action, women produced the conditions for full citizenship within the representational paradigm of democratic liberalism. Much broken glass and unladylike behavior punctuated these years. Historian Trevor Lloyd (1971) recounts how, in the year 1913, militant suffragettes "burnt a couple of rural railway stations ... placed a bomb in the house being built for [British Cabinet Minister] Lloyd George at Walton Heath in Surrey, and ... wrote 'Votes for Women' in acid on the greens of some golf courses." What's more, "these attacks were meant to hurt."

> Previously women who had been breaking the law, whether in a peaceful way or by marching in procession without police permission, or violently by breaking windows or trying to force their way into the Commons, had intended to be arrested in order to show that they took their beliefs seriously, and to make a speech from the dock in defense of their beliefs at the trial. But by [1913] the suffragettes were no longer looking for opportunities for martyrdom. They wanted to fight against society. (89)

Contemporary activists will recognize the transition outlined by Lloyd as bearing a striking resemblance to the recursive interval between the moment of civil disobedience and engagement in direct action.[31] It's therefore not surprising that, just as in other instances when protestors have moved from martyrdom to confrontation, the suffragettes' turn to militancy led to harsh criticism. Violent action, many suggested, annulled the benefits of mythic feminine status—that gift that "enabled" women to transcend dirty politics through ontological purity. By refusing the status of both victim and muse, the suffragette became nothing short of a political and symbolic anomaly. She appeared on the world stage by defiantly extricating herself from the rubble of a historic contradiction that has yet to be resolved. Producing a new and intelligible category from the nineteenth century antinomy between "Woman" and "the political" required decisive action. And so, even as they sought recognition from constituted power, the suffragettes nevertheless understood that "Woman" as representational category needed to be more than a myth, a muse, a node in the organization of consumption.

Through systematic and uproarious interjection, this new woman entered history not as an abstract universal but as a conscious actor—a force to be both recognized and reckoned with. According to historian Melanie Philllips, suffragettes like Teresa Billington-Greig began to recognize the ontological scope of their claims when their actions led them into direct conflict with the state. Sitting in Holloway prison for assaulting a cop at a demonstration, Billington-Greig concluded that, since women were denied the rights of citizenship, "logically they had to be outlaws and rebels" (2003: 182). Billington-Greig refused to testify at her trial, arguing that the court had no jurisdiction over those it did not—and could not—recognize as its citizens.

Reflecting on a similar feeling of ontological transformation a few years prior to Billington-Greig's arrest, Emmeline Pethick-Lawrence could not help but to feel inspired. Suffragette action had changed her: "Gone was the age-old sense of inferiority, gone the intolerable weight of helplessness in the face of material oppression... And taking the place of the old inhibitions was the release of powers that we had never dreamed of," she wrote (2003: 172). Despite the remarkable differences in their objective circumstances, Pethick-Lawrence expressed a sentiment that neatly anticipated the dynamite that Fanon would commit to paper 60 years later.[32] It's therefore not surprising that, according to Phillips, by 1908 "civil disobedience gave way to threats to public order." These included "destruction of property such as window-breaking and occasional violence against members of the government" (189).

During this period, many suffragettes argued that violence was not the antithesis of rights (as many liberals had claimed) but rather their *precondition*. This perspective resonated strongly with leading suffragette Christabel Pankhurst as she witnessed police break up a Manchester labor meeting assembled to address unemployment. Pankhurst concluded that it was only through violence that people would be recognized *as* people. From the perspective of the rights-granting state, violence seemed to be the precondition to political intelligibility (2003: 174). Arriving at similar conclusions, Frances Berkeley Young noted in 1912 that the actions of suffragettes conformed in every detail to England's cherished history of struggle for equal rights and liberal freedoms.

"Need I recall to any student of history," Young asked rhetorically, "the serious rioting and destruction of property which has preceded every advance in the liberties of which England is so proud" (cited in Neumann 2001: 111).

■

The history of the struggles against enclosure and for suffrage makes it possible to question the commonsense that draws logical correspondences between rioting and masculinity. By paying attention to the gender of rioters throughout the history of capitalism in the West, it becomes possible to dispel the myth that rioting has been a purely masculine pursuit. Correspondingly, though it might empirically be the case that women did far less rioting than did men at anti-summit actions, this cannot be said to be the result of some natural—or even some politically expedient—arrangement. Women have been rioters in the past. They have recognized the importance of rioting in pursuit of political objectives and even of political being. And while contemporary detractors of the Black Bloc have done their best to discredit the Bloc's actions as macho rabble rousing, the historic gender of the riot has been both masculine and feminine.

At the same time, the history of riots from the nineteenth century onward reveals the extent to which the meaning of the category "woman" underwent significant transformations as a result of the emergent relationship between violence and liberal democracy. As Rowbotham explains, "the new conception of commitment" that arose in moments of political violence "could upset what had been regarded as the women's sphere" (1974: 104). As a phenomenon pertaining to a way of being rather than to a prescribed content (as a concept that enabled people to adopt the standpoint of *the project* rather than that of a narrowly conceived interest), "commitment" became the vehicle for self-realization and becoming. In this formulation, committed people act on the basis of what their act demonstrably *produces* rather than on the basis of what it is thought to *mean* within a fixed frame of reference. Because the social organization of gender relied (and relies) extensively on the register of signification, the turn toward committed action (where recognition is demoted to a place of secondary importance) can be seen as an opening move in the war on gender itself.

As Rowbotham, Young, and others make clear, the history of riots against property and profit has been indelibly marked by women's participation. It's therefore not surprising to discover that (despite all claims to the contrary) women were active participants in anti-globalization riots as well. Writing about her experiences in the Black Bloc at demonstrations against the G8 meetings held in Genoa during August of 2001, "Mary Black" goes so far as to directly address the limitations of the riot = masculine equation:

> I think the stereotype is true that we are mostly young and mostly white, although I wouldn't agree that we are mostly men. When I'm dressed from head to toe in baggy black clothes, and my face is covered up, most people think I'm a man too. The behavior of Black Bloc protestors is not associated with women, so reporters often assume we are all guys. (Black 2001)

In her investigation of the ambiguous feminist character of the anti-globalization movement, Judy Rebick (2002) quotes activist Krystalline Kraus expressing a similar sentiment: "'Blocking up' to become the Black Bloc is a great equalizer. With everyone looking the same—everyone's hair tucked away, our faces obscured by masks, I'm nothing less and nothing more than one entity moving in the whole..." (Rebick 2002). However, as Kraus points out, this moment of release from the constraints of gender lasts only as long as the riot itself. Before and after the action, at public meetings and at the bar, movement debates continue to be the preserve of men. But if the riot is a "great equalizer" because of the exigencies of commitment, it's worth considering how it might also stand as the inaugural moment of a post-representational politics. If the contemporary riot brings with it a moment of gender abolition, where one becomes nothing more than "one entity moving in the whole," how might we extend its effects into regions of life where the logic of representation remains dominant? Can we enter the space opened up by the riot and never leave it?

■

Although it's been the subject of endless political debate, activists have often had difficulty clearly describing what they intend by "inclusion." Because it's an ontological and not a political category; because it tends to valorize the filiative bonds of present tense *being* over the affiliative impulses of future tense *becoming*; because, finally, it traces the movement of entities from spaces of exteriority into some predetermined inside, "inclusion" has posed real difficulties for radical politics.[33] Whether carried out in an aggregative fashion or (with more nuance) in an effort to induce an elected (and often predetermined) self-transformation, "inclusion" has often seemed to assume that the space of inclusion is itself a nearly perfect universal.

In opposition to this perspective, feminist writers concerned with anti-imperialist struggles have shown how inclusion has worked *against* political projects cognizant of the need to seize power and transform the world. Chandra Mohanty (1995) is unequivocal on this point in her assessment of Robin Morgan's mid-nineties call for a "planetary feminism." For Mohanty, the politics of inclusion inevitably leads to an abstract "universal sisterhood" (a condition that reiterates many of the features granted to Liberté). Although envisioned as a container into which all difference can be subsumed, Mohanty recounts how—in practice—"universal sisterhood" has disclosed an uncanny allegiance to the particular interests of white middle class women.

> Universal sisterhood, defined as the transcendence of the "male" world, thus ends up being a middle class, psychologized notion which effectively erases material and ideological power differences within and among groups of women, especially between First and Third World women (and, paradoxically, removes us all as actors from history and politics). (77)

Because it removes women from the political sphere, it's doubtful that "sisterhood" could provide the epistemic or tactical bases for resistance. As an abstract relation prompted by recognition of an equally abstract category, "inclusion of woman" necessitates that the category "woman" be given content. But who will be included? Because the moment of recognition becomes the moment of inscription, women who act in ways that exceed the normative grounds of the category cease to be intelligible. Or, to put it another way, since Morgan's "sisterhood" presupposes norms that are potentially antithetical to Krauss and Black's actions; since Krauss and Black seem to act like men and refuse to transcend the field of ruthless masculine politics, "sisterhood" may be left with no option but to expel them from its bounds.

Then again, in a moment of compromise, "sisterhood" might acknowledge the contradictions that arise from its aggregative constitution and make an exception. But what happens to a normative category that allows exceptions? At its logical limit, inclusion of exceptional content makes the category into which the content is subsumed wholly superfluous. By making the distinction between inside and outside (friend and enemy) impossible, "exceptional inclusion" of this kind ends by undermining the minimum requirements of political thought and action. Although inclusion brings with it a number of benefits (and here we might think of the possibility of forging a collective "we" *prior to* the resolution of contradictions within the assembled body), it also highlights a number of ontological lacunae that cannot be perpetually deferred.

By deferring the resolution of its ontological lacunae, contemporary feminism has been subject to an increasingly frequent return of the repressed. From Sojourner Truth to Audre Lorde, the history of feminist action has been shaped by confrontations with the limits of the category "woman." These confrontations have for the most part (and up until recently) taken the form of attempts to expand the category so as to include the experiences of those who had previously gone unrecognized. These efforts have been important. However, they bring with them the challenge of determining how to constitute a political "we" at the point where the distinction between inside and outside dissolves. This problem is surmountable; however, it requires that we recognize how the goal of inclusion is itself too narrow to encapsulate the opportunities signaled by the anti-globalization movement's riotous actions. These events highlighted a place where stable gender categories (and even genders themselves) might begin to fall apart.

■

In moments like the riot (in moments when people choose to reject, or fail to approximate, established norms), representational certainties begin to unravel. It's therefore not surprising to find media commentators, state officials, and (occasionally) activists themselves doing their utmost to make the new scene intelligible by inscribing the riot as male. The goal of this work is not "truth" but conceptual intelligibility. And with conceptual intelligibility comes the possibility of induction into the logic of ruling relations. As Mary Black points out, one of the most cherished gender norms applied to women—a norm applied with stunning regularity in both mainstream and popular feminist accounts—is that they are ontologically *anti-violent*. Because of this, recognizing women in the riot would mean destabilizing the intelligibility of the category "woman" itself.

In mainstream accounts, violence is often viewed as the natural preserve of men. Women are thus cast as victims incapable of mobilizing violence or as muses unwilling to consider it on account of their moral superiority. Given this restrictive framework, it has often been difficult for women to imagine using violence in order to accomplish goals—even when it can be demonstrated to be in their interest to do so. It's understandable that the patriarchal mainstream has sought, out of sheer self-interest, to make violence unthinkable for women. However, it's more difficult to grasp why this tendency has been such a recurrent feature of feminist thought.

Melanie Kaye/Kantrowitz (1992) has pointed out how dangerous the feminist love affair with the victim has been in light of the need to resist violence against women. While many women do not feel comfortable being violent, Kantrowitz notes, this should not be confused with the idea that women are *naturally* non-violent or that victim status is the only basis for political recognition. Women, she argues, have been systematically deprived of access to violence—first, by a masculine culture that declares violence to be its unique and sovereign entitlement, and second by a tendency within feminism to draw natural associations between violence and the oppressor. However, for Kantrowitz, "the idea that women are inherently non-violent is … dangerous because it is not true."

> Any doctrine that idealizes us as the non-violent sex idealizes our victimiza-
> tion and institutionalizes who men say we are: intrinsically nurturing, inher-
> ently gentle, intuitive, emotional. They think; we feel. They have power; we
> won't touch it with a ten-foot pole. Guns are for them; let's suffer in a special
> kind of womanly way. (24)

Why has it been difficult for feminists to imagine violence as a viable strategy for political transformation? Why, despite a documented history of women's violent struggle, have women tended to disavow their capacity for violence? Part of the answer can be found in the representational habit of positing resistance as the logical negation of the thing being resisted. In the case of violence, this means that—since men wield violence against women in an effort to maintain relations of domination—the use of violence by women would only serve to strengthen the logic of domination itself. Rachel Neumann confirms this tendency when she describes the feelings that some anti-globalization activists had with respect to the Black Bloc riot. In her account, protestor violence seems to reiterate existing power imbalances. "Property destruction," she notes, "has often been linked with larger uses of violence."

> Because of the way that men in particular are taught to repress and vent their
> anger, it often comes out as an exaggerated representation of masculinity,
> reproducing instead of contradicting the existing power structure. (111)

According to this logic, by using violence to smash the violent system, activists end by reinforcing the system itself. Here, violence is construed as a logical quantity, a sign that can only be negated by siding with its *representational* antithesis. But Neumann's formulation says more about the state of our current political impoverishment (where everything is subsumed within the representational sphere) than it does about violence itself. And while it can be easily transposed into the field of representation, violence itself is not merely a representational act. Its political effects can't be measured on a balance sheet of stable significations. By abstracting violence from its social context, by distilling it into a representational essence and disconnecting it from the world of lived experience, activists run the risk of foreclosing the possibility of even contemplating the political use of violence.

■

In order to justify violence's political inadmissibility, activists have sometimes made use of an idea popularized by Audre Lorde: "The master's tools will never dismantle the master's house" (1984: 110).[34] There is no doubt that maxims like these are seductive. However, they rarely provoke a material reckoning with the world. Which tools, precisely, *belong* to the master? Furthermore, how did these tools end up in his hands and not ours? Drawing upon a documented history of struggle, Kantrowitz points out that violence has been women's tool too. To make arguments to the contrary requires deliberate and exhausting self-deception (1992: 23). Worse, the urge to relinquish violence so as to avoid identity with the master reduces *social relations* to a constellation of abstract concepts and *resistance* to a process of conceptual negation. Such an orientation makes it nearly impossible to imagine a field of struggle that is not bound in advance by the claustrophobic universe of representational logic. Practically, it means that the consolidation of male power leads women toward ever-greater identification with the unattainable transcendental realm.

By positing violence wholly within the purview of a masculinist discourse of social domination, the inverse set of propositions is thus simultaneously secured: by virtue of being the antithetical term, to *be female* means defining oneself against dominant masculinist practice. Consequently, victimization becomes a central aspect (and defining feature) of the feminine. As a political figure, "Woman" thus becomes representationally coherent by way of her marginality and the restitution this condition solicits from constituted power.

Viewed as a hyperbolic representational negation (victim) or as an unachievable ideal (muse), "Woman" as we know her today indeed does not riot. History, however, contradicts this claim. In opposition to "Woman," *women* are demonstrably capable of enacting violent and powerful practices rather than simply being their victims.[35] Indeed, the history of violent political struggle since the 1960s is impossible to imagine without recalling the women who refused to be either victims or muses, who refused to live the proxy life of categorical abstraction.

Women's possibilities for asserting political power have diminished in inverse proportion to men's historical efforts to encapsulate politically power-ful practices within a normative and coherent masculine identity. Unless they adopt "common" tactics, women are left with few options but to valorize the antithetical term of the gender binary.[36] Of these two courses of action, only the former allows us to consider how appropriation of our adversary's tactics is not simply mimetic. Consequently, laying claim to the capacity for violence is not only about expanding women activists' arsenal of available tactics. It is, more pressingly, about provoking a breakdown in normative male/female gender designations and relations themselves.

Operating from a region of social subordination to both the state and to individual men, neither women in specific nor activists in general can afford to presume that "violence is violence," or that the "same thing" in a different context is really the same. Arguing against both the Stalinists and the bourgeois moralists of the 1930s, Leon Trotsky put it like this: "A slaveholder who through cunning and violence shackles a slave in chains, and a slave who through cunning and violence breaks the chains—let not the contemptible eunuchs tell us that they are equals before a court of morality" (1973: 38). "Contemptible eunuchs" notwithstanding, Trotsky encourages us to contemplate political action in a manner that shifts the focus from normative meaning to practical outcome.

Considered in light of our present argument, Trotsky's position amounts to a commitment to resistance coordinated from the standpoint of power-ful social practices rather than from within the predetermined borders of a socially-constituted female subjectivity. Following the argument one step further, we must conclude (along with Trotsky) that those who fawn "over the precepts established by the enemy will never vanquish that enemy" (45). At this point, it becomes clear that the "precept" is *not* violence (which is normally taken to be the *preserve* and not the *precept* of the enemy) but the category "woman" itself.

We can therefore re-read Lorde's maxim recognizing that, as a tool, the moral precept—the constellation of established normative meanings that reaf-firm the status quo—will indeed never dismantle the master's house. The vio-lence of conceptual abstraction conceals the concrete violence of the everyday world. Nevertheless, it remains evident that the state's laws cannot be used to abolish the state any more than the production of commodities for profit can ever emancipate the producer.

The implication here is not, as has sometimes been claimed, that women must act "like men" in order to wield violence. Rather, it is that—by appropriating means of powerful political assertion to which they've historically been denied recourse—women tell the lie of the normative masculine identification with power. In *Gender Trouble*, Butler points out how a women's repetition of a practice currently encoded as male can have the effect of transforming both the practice and the actor into something new. "To operate within the matrix of power is not the same as to replicate uncritically relations of domination," she says. "It offers the possibility of a repetition of the law which is not its consolidation, but its displacement" (1990: 30). Women's participation in the Black Bloc suggests as intriguing vector of displacement in Butler's sense.

■

Other parallels can be drawn. As a moment of unmediated engagement with history, the riot breaks down individual certainties and encourages the formation of post-representational political subjectivities. In this respect, the riot provides a concrete expression of the disruptions anticipated by the surrealist insurgency that punctuated the early twentieth century. Searching for an avenue along which to launch an assault on the conceptual mystifications of the bourgeoisies, Walter Benjamin proposed in 1929 that—despite its lack of political clarity—surrealism could reconnect people with a zone of experience where things and their names would begin to correspond more directly.

"In the world's structure," he posits, "dream [the surrealist's currency] loosens individuality like a bad tooth. This loosening of the self by intoxication is, at the same time, precisely the fruitful, living experience that allowed these people to step outside the domain of intoxication" (1978: 179). Like in Krauss's account of her Black Bloc experience, where the tactical exigencies of the riot make a member of the Black Bloc "nothing less and nothing more than one entity moving in the whole," Benjamin's analysis emphasizes surrealism's assault on the representational subject certainties of modern individuality. By passing through the deconstitutive moment, these figures initially intoxicated by dream reach a point of ecstatic clarity. The violent immediacy of the act thus stands as precondition to the production of the critical distance required for mediated analysis. Once unthinkable, the riot produces circumstances in which people begin to change themselves in the process of changing the world.

There are still other possibilities. Readers familiar with Frantz Fanon will undoubtedly recognize the dynamic under consideration as being similar to the one that he recounts in *The Wretched of the Earth*. In that book, Fanon (1963) describes how the native, upon passing through violence, takes history into his own person and, in the process, rediscovers the capacity to *be* political. Liberation is made possible by considering avenues that come into view only after the colonized choose that which had previously been unthinkable. Standing at the threshold between the thinkable and the unthinkable is violence. "At the level of the individual," Fanon claims, "violence is a cleansing force."

> It frees the native from his inferiority complex and from his despair and inaction; it makes him fearless and restores his self-respect... The action which has thrown them into a hand-to-hand struggle confers upon the masses a voracious taste for the concrete. (94–95)

This "taste for the concrete" moves the newly historicized political subject beyond the realm of representation. Violence rematerializes the world and its social relations. No longer do the oppressed seek the recognition of the colonizer. Their claims to freedom do not need his approval. In his introduction to Fanon's work, Jean-Paul Sartre marveled at the way the anti-colonial struggle had changed the Algerians' outlook: Europe was sinking but they didn't care. All of this confirmed that they were *becoming political*.

Theoretical considerations and histories of struggle like the ones recounted above will undoubtedly seem remote from the experiences of privileged political contenders that, like the ACME collective, descended on the streets of Seattle in 1999. Nevertheless, from the standpoint of *epistemology*, a very similar process to the one described by Fanon was at work in the anti-globalization riot. Many participants seemed to experience mass anti-summit actions as a date with history, an unmediated moment in which they become fully invested in the consequentiality of their actions.[37]

In addition to the ground clearing made possible by ecstatic action, the anti-globalization riot made a further break with representational politics by not advancing particular demands, by *not asking for anything*. State officials, whether politicians or police, frequently complained that anti-globalization activists were a cacophonous bunch. They did not seek to meet with leaders; they did not seek particular reforms. They did not even seek positive media coverage—and not infrequently did they attack the vehicles of corporate media outlets. Like a tormented parent dealing with a recalcitrant child, state officials were left to cry out in exasperation: "What do you *want?*"

The anti-globalization riot served as a means to break with the representational paradigm in one final way. Because of their task-oriented sensibilities (their "commitment," in Rowbotham's sense), activists—and this was most true of those who used the Black Bloc tactic—tended toward a uniform appearance that made recognition difficult. Starting from the standpoint of the task, rioters selected appropriate tools and clothes. As with their historic counterparts the Whiteboys, the practical consequence of activist commitment was sartorial uniformity. And, as in the past, emphasis fell not on what the uniform *meant* but rather on what it *enabled.*

■

Because it emphasized engaged and unmediated participation; because it broke with the politics of demand enshrined in democratic liberalism; because it placed emphasis on the politics of the act, where participants aimed to produce their truths directly, the anti-globalization riot uncovered a space where women might cause the kind of gender trouble esteemed by Butler. By helping to destabilize gender categories, rioting women prefigure a world in which the political-representational matrix of gender (where identity is the precondition for both subjectivity and regulation) begins to lose its salience. Even as a hypothesis, such a proposition is worthy of sustained consideration—not least because it provides a means of moving radical politics from its current focus on gender inclusion toward the more radical perspective of gender abolition.

Rather than seeking to *include* women, activists might use the riot to abolish "woman" as a significant social category. In the process, the category "man"—a category made intelligible only through its binary opposition to "woman"—is also desecrated. Feminists have contemplated this possibility before. In "The Accentuation of Female Appearance," early twentieth century American feminist Laura (Riding) Jackson (1993) pointed out that, even though women of her period had begun to extend their activities into what had previously been male domains, they also began to aesthetically emphasize their femininity. As the distinctions between men and women began to break down in the sphere of practical activity, they became increasingly codified in the sphere of representation. As "the female role becomes more and more extended," Jackson noted.

the dramatic duality of woman becomes more and more emphatic. And this duality is not only insisted on by women; it is equally insisted on by man. For if woman, as such, disappears from the drama, the drama itself collapses." (114)

In this case, disappearing "as such" from the drama meant disentangling oneself from the binds of signification. Alternative representations, though they are often important, can only change *what* people perceive. In contrast, by abolishing representational distinctions through productive practices, activists could foster a radical break with the representational paradigm underlying contemporary ruling regimes. In this way, they could contribute to changing *how* people perceive.

More immediately, breaking with the representational paradigm challenges the centrality of identity to contemporary politics. These politics, although important for the developments they've entailed, have never been without contradiction. And, as most activists will attest, these contradictions have often been immobilizing. But while there have been numerous content-based critiques of identity politics over the last twenty years, it took Butler to point out how identity—since it provides the basis for social recognition—is itself a regulatory practice.

In *Gender Trouble*, Butler asks: "what kind of subversive repetition might call into question the regulatory practice of identity itself" (1990: 32). Although she does not consider it, women's participation in the Black Bloc is such a repetition. By circumventing the representational sphere and attacking the epistemic basis of political identity, and by recasting politics as a practice of production rather than one of signification, Black Bloc women anticipate a moment beyond the recognition-regulation matrix of today's society of control.

To be clear, since they begin from within it, Black Bloc rioters cannot pretend to possess a tidy means of transcending representational stipulations. However, their practices do seem to unsettle some of these stipulations' most cherished principles. By emphasizing unmediated engagement, a critical approach to the politics of demand, and a celebration of the act, the rioters' commitment makes gender representation (and hence gender itself) less tenable. And so, while anti-globalization riots were not always tactically efficacious, their significance may in fact reside elsewhere. And so, while it doesn't accord with the disciplined messaging of contemporary movements, we must keep the possibility of gender abolition in mind as we enter the next cycle of struggle. To the extent that this possibility was made visible during the anti-globalization movement, it stood as a meaningful prefiguration of the world we are struggling to create.

In this world, we can imagine subjects without identities and politics unbound by the stale conventions of recognition. These politics are made possible by a violent assault on conceptual abstraction and—their capitalist outgrowth—property relations. This is especially the case when conducted by a "woman" who is herself a conceptual outgrowth of those very relations. Most importantly, these politics anticipate a people who will exist whether or not we are represented. Through our activity, the world itself will confirm our being.

CHAPTER FIVE

THE COMING CATASTROPHE

T he optimism was short-lived. By the time of the demonstrations against the WTO mini-ministerial meetings in Montreal in July of 2003, many of the activists with whom I had worked since 1999 had become disenchanted with the themes and sensibilities of anti-globalization. The promotional materials for the demo read "Mini-Ministerial? Mega Protest!" But though the action had been called with the noble goal of disrupting the meetings of elite WTO members who would try to ram through their agenda in Cancun later that year, fewer than 1000 people turned up for the day of disruption. The spokescouncil meeting the night before the action seemed like a formality. As a result of both serious tactical mistakes and low numbers, the demonstration ended in failure. Activists could not get close to the heavily fortified hotel in which the meeting was taking place. Disruption would have to wait for another day.[38]

As demonstrators gathered along the perimeter of the hotel, the police sprang into action. The protest was declared an "illegal assembly" and riot cops quickly formed into tight lines. The demonstrators were forced to flee. It seemed rehearsed. It seemed inevitable. Moving with far greater discipline and precision than the assembled activists, the police effectively neutralized the protest by threatening to engulf it.

The whole scene was a grim mixture of determination and despair. After running through parking lots and alleys to avoid the police mousetrap, the activists—panting and out of breath—gathered haphazardly on Rue St.

Catherine and began smashing windows. A Canadian Armed Forces recruiting office, a multi-national fast food joint, and a sweatshop boutique were quickly targeted. The police followed closely behind. In another context, the sound of broken glass hitting concrete may have been uplifting. But on that day, there was something desperate about the sharp clinking. It didn't have the ring that it did in Seattle. Besides, since activists did not have control of the streets on that morning (since, let's face it, we were on the run), we were hardly in a position to sit around and admire—let alone critique—our handiwork.

Taking their cue from the demonstrators' disorganization and blatant illegality, the police moved in and once again dispersed the crowd. Those unlucky enough not to find an escape route were arrested. Over a crackling megaphone, organizers told the rest of us to reassemble in the "green zone" outside of the anarchist bookstore on the other side of town. With little else planned for the morning, many activists headed in that direction. It was still before 9am. Over the next hour, activists slowly gathered in the parking lot beside the bookstore and tried to make sense of the morning's failures. Others, more ambitious, tried to figure out what would happen next. The answer was less than a block away. Once again, the police encircled—this time with a solid line of riot cops in every direction. A few activists, fleet of foot, managed to escape. Most, however, became trapped.

For the rest of the morning, I stood around with a group of protestors who had managed to escape and watched as nearly two hundred activists were slowly taken into custody on charges of "participating in a riot." The ridiculous nature of the charge was of little comfort. It was bad enough that these activists would have to spend time in police custody and hire lawyers for charges that weren't going to stick. But the humiliation of *seeking* to riot—as some activists undoubtedly had—and not being able to (the humiliation of facing riot charges in abstention of any real action): now *that* was heartbreaking.

■

The movement lost in Montreal. From this experience, many activists with whom I had been working concluded that the anti-globalization movement's mode of organizing (to say nothing of its infantile and unswerving optimism) no longer matched political conditions. It was easy to see their point. The police had learned to contain us more quickly than we had learned to become uncontainable. Perhaps most sobering, however, was how the movement's enthusiasm for ecstatic personal freedom and unmediated action did not match the post-September 11 reality of torture, expedited deportations, and attacks on communities of color.

Considered alongside the failed action against the mini-ministerial meeting, the preceding day's No One is Illegal march seemed to be by far the greater success. This was true in spite of the difficulties faced on that day. Although it was larger than the anti-WTO action that would follow, the No One Is Illegal march was still smaller than many activists had hoped. And, as if to take pathetic fallacy to new levels, rain began to fall in torrents as activists passed in front of the immigration office. Many thus sought shelter beneath its awning and in front of its locked doors. But despite these minor setbacks, organizers could point to the alliances that they were helping to build between the predominantly white anti-globalization scene and members of targeted communities. Palestinians, Algerians, anti-capitalist students, and *lumpen* street punks all on the same page: now that was something you could build on.

The people who smashed windows during the anti-WTO action didn't fit the caricature of the disenchanted middle class white kid associated with the anti-globalization movement. But this did not prevent many activists from attributing the action's shortcomings to this figure's purported lack of political sophistication. Organizing work is hard, some pointed out soberly. And though it might be cathartic (though it might be a release for those with little sense of collective responsibility), the impulse to petty destruction cannot be confused with meaningful politics. This was especially the case, others added, in light of the changing terrain of global politics. Marked indelibly by hyperbolic bombast and a hail of bombs, imperialist war meant that it was time for activists to grow up.

Underlying these critiques was a renunciation of the belief that anti-globalization violence had unleashed new political possibilities. In another time, the distance between advocates of militant action and their detractors was mediated and moderated by the slippery call for a "respect for a diversity of tactics." However, under the new conditions (and with the movement in Canada and the US in a precipitous state of decline), activists who had been uncomfortable with property destruction began to advance their arguments with greater force: Montreal showed that politics could not start from the gut. Marshaling energy was not the same thing as producing results. The urge to destroy (however humanizing it might feel given the depravity of the hated world) could not be confused with the more important work of organizing. And anyway, the focus on "tactics" that had pervaded the movement had the fundamental weakness of self-absorption. What could the violent temper tantrum of a black-clad punk bent on smashing in a window mean to someone with real problems?

■

Then as now, these criticisms all need to be taken seriously. What they fail to consider, however, is the role that violence has played in the creation of new people. The white and middle class character of the anti-globalization movement may have been annoying, but this doesn't mean that it wasn't in the middle of an important process of transformation at the moment it was prematurely cut short. And so, while the movement's experiments with violence were strategically inconclusive (to say the least), they nevertheless marked an important moment of becoming through which white middle class dissidents glimpsed the possibility of reconnecting with the political sphere. And it's only after reconnecting with politics that these dissidents would have been able to forge meaningful coalitions with those facing the blunt force of neo-liberal capital accumulation.

While it has not always been tactically efficacious from the standpoint of movement objectives, a brief look at history reveals that violence has always been a factor in the genesis of new forms of political subjectivity. Because of this, calls to "non-violence," regardless of their motivation, fail on two counts: first, because—as a species of abstract and representational negation—they do not deal with the fact of violence *per se*; second, because the ability to act politically (up to and including the ability to make exhortations about the need to act non-violently) is itself founded on violence. By turning violence into a logical abstraction that can in turn be abstractly refuted, calls to non-violence ignore the most basic elements of the relationship between ontology, violence, and politics.

The relationship is this: violence turns ontology into politics. It is the catalyst that intensifies being and transposes it into the register of becoming. Refusing, or failing to acquire, the means to be violent amounts to an agreement to remain as we are. However, this agreement does not escape violence; it simply defers to the violence of those who constituted the inherited situation. These dynamics can be seen at work both within the razor wire world described by Fanon in *The Wretched of The Earth* and within the matrix of western biopower with which anti-globalization activists were infinitely more familiar.[39] In both instances, despite obvious differences in the content of experience, the facts of ontological transformation remain the same. In both cases, the challenge is to seize violence and to make the transformation it entails political; it means making it a site of activist intervention and putting it at the center of our project. Most of all, it means not abandoning it in moments when it ceases to appear expedient.

■

The difficulty with thinking about violence as the threshold between ontology and politics arises, in part, from the fact that discussions about violence within movements often approach the question from the standpoint of its representational transposition. Here, violence-as-signifier is read against "non-violence," its purported antithesis. What this framing misses are the stakes. Will the dissident be a representation or a production? Will she act at the level of the signifier or the signified? Will she change what people think about the world or will she change the world itself? Although many activists have valorized "non-violence" as a productive principle, it discloses (in its very formulation) a tacit recognition that violence itself is the positive term. While violence pertains to production, avowals of "non-violence" function principally through representational negation. In contrast to the negative ethical implications of "non-violence" (where the subject seeks to preserve the world's existent forms), violence impels actors to consider how the world's forms might be transformed for the better through productive action. What already is, it can be said, is never enough.

For this reason, it makes little sense to engage with violence as an ethical problem. Since ethics can only be convincingly elaborated in relation to choice, and since—from the standpoint of what-already-is—non-violence amounts to a choosing-not-to-choose, both ethics and violence are left to find their true reference point in the production process. Still, it's been difficult for many thinkers to attribute a productive role to violence. In her response to the New Left's growing endorsement of violence, Hannah Arendt took pains to point out how—despite the conviction that he championed bloodshed—Marx did not see violence as the engine of social change. According to Arendt, "Marx was aware of the role of violence in history, but this role was to him secondary; not violence but the contradictions inherent in the old society brought it to its end" (1970: 11).

In my view, Arendt was right to critique the activist tendency to fetishize violence. However, in so doing, she neglected the possibility that violence itself was *one of the contradictions inherent in the old society*. Instead of grappling with this obvious possibility (which once again places violence at the center of the relationship between ontology and politics), Arendt becomes engrossed with (and fundamentally misreads) Marx's metaphors of gestation. "The emergence of a new society was preceded, but not caused, by violent outbreaks, which he likened to the labor pangs that precede, but of course do not cause, the event of organic birth" (11).

But what if, rather than being an instrument (as Arendt insisted), violence was instead conceived as the site of struggle itself? According to Max Weber, one of the defining characteristics of the state is its ability to monopolize the legitimate use of violence. If this is the case, then we must conclude that a new society characterized by a democratization of violence (a democratization that coincides with the democratization of the means of production and can only be achieved alongside it) would amount to an abolition of the state.

Traced to its endpoint, this train of thought leads to a stunning possibility: violence, emancipated from the barbarism of its partial realization, becomes the basis for an emancipated people. It is the sentinel guarding the door between ontology and politics, between bare life and a post-human experience only hinted at in Walter Benjamin's conception of the proletariat's "weak messianic power." But despite its obvious connections to production, Arendt remained dogmatic in her insistence that violence be relegated to a separate and debased sphere of human activity. In her essay, violence is effectively quarantined from "thought" and "labor," those authentic categories underlying the modern German philosophical tradition.

> According to Hegel, man "produces" himself through thought, whereas for Marx, who turned Hegel's "idealism" upside down, it was labor, the human form of metabolism with nature, that fulfilled this function... It cannot be denied that a gulf separates the essentially peaceful activities of thinking and laboring from all deeds of violence... If one turns the "idealistic" concept of thought upside down, one might arrive at the "materialistic" concept of labor; one will never arrive at the notion of violence. (12–13)

Why the separation? From a phenomenological perspective, violence is virtually indistinguishable from labor: both are coordinated acts of becoming that simultaneously transform the producer and the world; both confirm the producer to the extent that the world is made her object. And let's not forget the violence implicit in every labor process. As every ecologist knows, "the human form of metabolism with nature" is hardly innocent. Even when approached with an eye trained on sustainability, the transformation of the world through production is violent *by definition*. And, unless we're willing to disavow production as such (as some fringe elements of today's primitivist movement have attempted to do), we must concede that the goal should not be to disavow violence but rather to ask: "what must we produce so that living in this world does not kill us?"

■

To concretize the connection between violence and production, it's useful to consider what took place during the American Civil War when the process of ontological transformation and the development of new political subjectivities were raw and on the surface. Despite the fact that Northerners were officially going to war in the name of ending slavery, they nevertheless expressed serious reservations about Blacks fighting for their own liberation. According to Melanie Kaye/Kantrowitz (1992), many Northern whites felt significant fear when confronted with the consequences of a genuine liberation struggle.

Some expressed this fear indirectly by claiming, for instance, that Blacks would prove to be incompetent and, as such, would not succeed in assuming the responsibilities of freedom. According to this perspective, arms given to Blacks fighting for the abolition of slavery would inevitably end up in rebel hands. But this line of reasoning did little to conceal the underlying and more serious anxiety: what if Blacks proved to be competent? A whole new arrangement would be required. At its inception, the Northern struggle to end slavery still pertained conceptually to an object relation. However, through the course of the violent struggle itself, it became clear that a new political subject—the Free Black—was illuminating the horizon of American politics. This fact could not help but be unsettling to those who had hitherto imagined that they were the benevolent custodians of a world of objects.

As an organized social force capable of soldier discipline, Blacks produced serious anxiety. If they could be soldiers, surely they could legitimate their demands for unqualified recognition of their worth. The appropriation of the capacity for (and the assertion of an entitlement to) violence—even in its most orderly and subservient military pose—yielded a new political arrangement from the very contradictions of American race politics. "Blacks felt pride, whites felt fear," Kantrowitz notes. "Both groups recognized that consciousness changed radically when the Black division marched through" (1992: 23).

In moments such as these, it became evident that violence was not freedom's antithesis. It was its precondition.

■

The kind of limited transformation experienced by white middle class dissidents during their struggles against corporate globalization has historical antecedents. Perhaps the greatest account of such a process can be found in Frantz Fanon's *Wretched of the Earth*, a book in which the connection between ontology, violence, and politics is made explicit. However, lest activists dismiss the possibility that their lives share anything with the situation described by Fanon (or that those struggling with the contradictions arising from a superabundance of social privilege might find their bearings by considering the structures underlying the conditions of oppression), there are other reference points to consider as well. American history is filled with countless instances of violent struggle in which the stakes included the capacity to assert oneself as a political being. Among these struggles, it's useful here to highlight Noel Ignatiev's research on the lives of Irish immigrants in the nineteenth century as they struggled to secure citizenship, political recognition, and, ultimately, white status.

In choosing these two seemingly antithetical examples (where one documents the struggle to attain liberation and the other traces the tragic movement of an oppressed group in its struggle to become white), my goal is to emphasize phenomenological similarities. Admittedly, the *content* of these transformations could not be more different; one is a break with colonial rule while the other is stark collusion. However, when considered from the standpoint of the transition from ontology to politics made possible by violence, they bear an uncanny resemblance to one another. And it's precisely this transition that we must consider when evaluating our own relationship to violence. The process is unwieldy and without guarantees. But the stakes are high. And it must not be forgotten that not acting also amounts to a decision.

In *The Wretched of the Earth*, Fanon draws an explicit connection between the capacity to produce social change through violence and acquiring what (following Aimé Césaire) he calls a human soul. Through violence, Fanon's colonized undergo a dramatic transformation in which they cease to be objects at the mercy of historical circumstance and become history's privileged actors. At the moment of this transformation, the colonized come to embody historical contradictions within their own person and make decisions based on these contradictions. Here, the measure of the human soul is its capacity to decide, to take risks in pursuit of that which is more than itself, and to stand unflinchingly before these actions as their final arbiter.

This process of becoming is not an abstract appeal to untapped human potential. It does not require a normative assumption of what it means to be human in order to operate. Instead, it begins from where the colonized begin and initially takes the form of a refusal. The content of this refusal is nothing but the negation of what it refuses. Nevertheless, it's only with this interruption (an interruption without content) that it becomes possible for production to begin on a new basis. And it's the precisely inhuman character of human production (the way that production demands extension of the self beyond the self through decisive action) that allows us to envision politics at all.

It's on this basis that we can understand Fanon's claim that the timeframe of decolonization is immediate. It is "the replacement of one species of men with another." This formulation is ordinarily read in reference to the process by which the colonized take the place of the colonizer and make him "superfluous." However, this "replacement" applies equally well to the colonized themselves. For, in the act of uprising, the colonized replace their prior selves with a subject *who did not yet exist* at the onset of violence.

Hannah Arendt objected to this emphasis on immediacy. If decolonization was truly immediate, Arendt contended, then this would mean that Fanon had effectively collapsed the distinction between violence and politics and made them indistinguishable. However, what this criticism overlooks are the basic preconditions of politics itself. As Ato Sekyi-Otu has pointed out, in the immediacy of the colonial encounter, "'the language of pure violence' is conspicuous by its '*immediate presence*.'"

> That is why it is grossly erroneous for critics such as Hannah Arendt to suppose that Fanon equates politics with violence. On the contrary, he is saying with the most classical of political philosophers that where there is no public space, there is no political relationship, only violence, "violence in the state of nature." "Concerning Violence" tells us that a social order in which the existential positions are implacably fixed in spaces by virtue of racial membership violates the minimum requirement of political association. "The politics of race"? Now, *that*, "Concerning Violence" seems to be saying, is an oxymoron. (86–87)

Here, once more, we can see how violence must precede politics. Or, put another way, it is the violent act that makes politics possible. When the historical cessation entailed by colonialism's anti-dialectic of pure violence is interrupted by the reciprocal violence of the colonized, the transition from ontology to politics is experienced as immediate. A space opens up, and the field is reconstituted as a contest between claimants who did not exist prior to the onset of violence. The context in which Fanon described this process was one of colonial constraint. Nevertheless, it's possible to identify the same dynamic in the context of western biopower. Definitive attributes of this condition include expulsion from the political field and the feeling that consequence and temporality have given way to the unbearable duration and an endless present. But before turning to an exploration of these conditions, it's first necessary to consider the means by which the immediate, anti-dialectical moment of colonization—a moment characterized by pure violence—might be overcome.

■

According to Fanon, decolonization is initially marked by a violent refusal. Consequently, the consciousness that shapes its initial expression is mapped onto an inherited dividing line. Since the colonized world is a world cut in two, the initial impulse of decolonization is to transcend the Manichean divide and obliterate those on the other side. Although "it is the settler who has brought the native into existence" (36), the native comes to realize that she has no need for her creator. Ostensibly in control, but ultimately dependent upon those he subordinates, the settler has dug his own grave.

In the process, the dividing line upon which the colonized first act (the dividing line that shaped consciousness in the first instance) becomes nothing more than a starting point. All that it lacks in political sophistication becomes clear as the struggle proceeds. Nevertheless, it remains the precondition to all that follows. "As we see it," says Fanon, "it is a whole material and moral universe which is breaking up… Thus the native discovers that his life, his breath, his beating heart are the same as those of the settler… All the new, revolutionary assurance of the native stems from it" (44–45).

Once these changes have taken place at the level of consciousness (once the colonized becomes free to move in a political fashion), the inherited dividing line ceases to serve the function it initially did. Once the anti-colonial struggle has moved through the realm of immediate violence and into the field of mediated politics, a profound shift begins to occur. According to Fanon, through the process of political struggle, "many members of the mass of colonialists reveal themselves to be much, much nearer to the national struggle than certain sons of the nation" (146).

In this way, the spontaneity of the first instance cedes to a kind of mediated political discernment that would have been impossible at the moment of the first rupture. "The barriers of blood and race prejudice are broken down on both sides," says Fanon. "In the same way, not every Negro or Moslem is issued automatically a hallmark of genuineness; and the gun or the knife is not inevitably reached for when a settler makes his appearance" (146). By passing *through* violence, the colonized move from ontology to politics. Consciousness moves from the immediate to the mediated. The political imagination moves from representational negation to production.

What emerges from this process did not exist prior to colonization. In this sense, anti-colonial violence is not *redemptive* in the conventional sense; it does not signal a return to origins or to some prior moment. However, at the same time, because it orients to the unfulfilled *promise* of the past, the anti-colonial struggle expresses a redemptive impulse by seeking to realize that promise in the present. The myth becomes productive. But even though a mythic connection to the past often guides the actions of the anti-colonial resistance, this past is itself marked by indeterminacy. It is a site of contestation. According to Fanon, many of the elders amongst the colonized seek to reconcile the contradictions of the moment just prior to decolonization by immersing themselves in the rituals of an anachronistic spirituality. However, for the younger generation, this solution seems doomed and is condemned from the outset:

> The youth of a colonized country, growing up in an atmosphere of shot and fire, may well make a mock of, and does not hesitate to pour scorn upon the zombies of his ancestors, the horses with two heads, the dead who rise again, and the djinns who rush into your body while you yawn. The native discovers reality and transforms it into the pattern of his customs, into the practice of violence and into his plans for freedom. (58).

Although he disavows the myths of his elders, the young anti-colonial fighter does not refrain from calling upon myth to animate his "plans for freedom." These myths take the form of stories about the heroes of past resistance struggles. They are conjured not so that the new insurgents might valorize themselves by claiming a dignified genealogy but because they are a useful means of provoking action. "The great figures of the colonized people," Fanon notes, "are always those who led the national resistance to invasion."

> Behanzin, Soundiata, Samory, Abdel Kader—all spring to life again with
> peculiar intensity in the period which comes directly before action. This is
> proof that the people are getting ready to move forward again, to put an end
> to the static period begun by colonization, and to make history. (69)

Accounts of violence such as this one can sometimes seem seductive.
However, the decisive moment marked by violence is only the gate through
which the subject must pass in order to regain the capacity to act politically.
And while it is a necessary first step, it does not contain its own content. The
question of *politics*, then, is inevitably this: *what will be produced in the space
opened up by violence?* Dissidents have not always been prepared to pose this
question. The intoxicating dimensions of violence have sometimes made it
difficult for its adherents to consider what comes next.

It was precisely for this reason that Hannah Arendt objected to New
Leftists who never seemed to read beyond the first chapter of *The Wretched
of the Earth*. Indeed, without taking account of "Spontaneity: Its Strengths
and Weaknesses" and "The Pitfalls of National Consciousness," Fanon's text
can seem like a quasi-religious or messianic injunction. It's in opposition to
this limited reading that I reiterate that the violence of the anti-globalization
movement (like that of the colonized) is merely the precondition—the first
step—toward the political. It is the price of entering the game.

■

If Fanon's story is one in which the oppressed learn through violence to define
themselves in terms that render the colonizer "superfluous," Noel Ignatiev's
story of Irish ascendance to white status in America outlines the same process
but with reverse valuations. Central to Ignatiev's analysis is the recognition
that, while the Irish in nineteenth century America were considered racially
inferior to whites and (in some instances) even more debased than Blacks,[40]
they had the advantage of never having been slaves (140). As such, they were
able to participate in acts of public violence in defense of their perceived interests as workers. In many instances, these actions took the form of mob
violence against Blacks. Ignatiev describes one such riot that took place in
Philadelphia in August of 1834:

> The mob ... marched down to South Street, to the adjacent township of
> Moyamensing, attacked a home occupied by a black family, and continued

its violence on the small side streets where the black people mainly lived. On Wednesday evening a crowd wrecked the African Presbyterian Church on Seventh Street and a place several blocks away called the "Diving Bell"... After reducing these targets to ruins, the rioters began smashing windows, breaking down doors, and destroying furniture in private homes of Negroes, driving the inmates naked into the streets and beating any they caught. (125)

Through their participation in race riots against Blacks in Philadelphia and elsewhere, Irish immigrants secured access to some of the entitlements of citizenship as they were conceived in nineteenth century America. In this context (a context that Ignatiev, following Machiavelli, fittingly describes as a "tumultuous republic"), the rights of the citizen were "distinguished by three main privileges: he could sell himself piecemeal; he could vote; and he could riot" (132). These rights were not taken lightly, and the riot came to play a crucial role in the development of American public affairs. As Ignatiev points out, "The urban riot was a common occurrence in the Jacksonian period."

One historian found that at least seventy percent of American cities with over 20,000 people experienced some major disorder in the 1839–65 period. Another counted thirty-five major riots in Baltimore, Philadelphia, New York and Boston from 1830 to 1860. The year 1834 alone saw sixteen riots, and the following year thirty-seven. No less a witness than Abraham Lincoln warned in 1837 that "accounts of outrages committed by mobs form the every-day news of the times." (131)

In the absence of a fully formed repressive state apparatus,[41] public sentiment and public policy were closely linked. Or, to put it another way, "disorder on such scale becomes order" (131). Or, again: "in that kind of extreme democracy, official response could not be separated from public opinion" (133). Despite the fact that they were motivated by a profoundly racist impulse, the "extreme democracy" of these riots bears a striking resemblance—at the level of form—to the kernel of truth underlying radical political projects. Indeed, the idea that democracy is best expressed by the will of the crowd in the street was a feature of the nineteenth century race riot just as surely as it was a feature of anti-globalization protests at the beginning of the twenty-first century. As Ignatiev recounts, a correspondent to a Philadelphia newspaper of the time defended a mob that attacked a Black establishment by appealing to revolutionary authority. "There was a law that authorized the destruction of the very tabernacle of abolitionism," the correspondent wrote. "The law was made on the spot—the very act was the law'" (136).

Just beneath the surface of this extreme democracy, however, the state was slowly and incrementally developing its repertoire of regulation and control. Drawing upon the energy of the violence in its midst, the state began cultivating its sovereign and biopolitical capacities. Key to this process was denying Blacks the right to self-defense. As Ignatiev explains, "only black people were excluded from equal participation in the war of each against all, and in restricting them to nonresistance the leaders of the tumultuous, white republic found the secret to government" (139).

By restricting Blacks to "nonresistance," the state was able to assume a mediating role—acting as a brake on white violence even as it effectively drew upon and represented this violence through institutional forms. In the process, the space for unmediated and unpredictable street violence was significantly curbed. By asserting its absolute power to declare the exception, the emergent state ensured that the tumultuous republic slowly became orderly. In no way did this "order" decrease the amount of racist hostility toward Blacks. However, it did mean that the Irish (who had once been outside of the constraints of white respectability) were now effectively bound by its stipulations. Whiteness itself became characterized by a willingness to be represented by, and defer to, the state. As we've seen, deference has been especially acute for the white middle class. Throughout the course of the twentieth century, the unanimity of their deferral gradually pushed them out of the political field altogether.

Presenting these case studies in this way runs the risk of suggesting that they denote equivalent experiences of suffering. To be clear: no analogy can be drawn between the political repression endured by the colonized and the relatively minor indignities endured by anti-globalization activists. On the other hand, while some commentators have argued that the anti-globalization movement was implicitly racist, this racism does not match—in either deliberation or scale—the racism expressed by the nineteenth century Irish Americans considered by Ignatiev. If we add to these differences the fact that anti-globalization activists were for the most part able to select the conflicts in which they became ensnared, the basis for comparison becomes even smaller.

What does remain common to each instance, however, is the fact of transformation. In all three cases (though far less so in the case of the anti-globalization movement, which remained an incomplete experiment whose promise has yet to be realized), what emerged at the end could not have come into being without first having passed through violence. This transformation, which can be measured by considering the new forms of political subjectivity it yields, can be analyzed and operationalized by movements striving to become political. As Ignatiev's study confirms, this transformation is not necessarily or inevitably radical. However, if activists do not make violence the site of their political genesis, they effectively cede it to those who will. The results, I submit, aren't pretty.

■

For Fanon, violence provided the colonized with a means of calling into question the logic of a world "strewn with prohibitions." In contrast, Ignatiev recounted how crowd violence became the means by which the state gained the capacity to assert its sovereignty, increase its regulatory function, and fashion an orderly republic. On the surface, these two outcomes suggest that the effects of violence are open-ended and contradictory. But despite this ambivalence, there are also profound points of connection between Ignatiev's and Fanon's accounts. Both examples point to the sovereign state as the principal means by which violence is contained and channeled. Further, both examples show the profound interconnection between forms of rule and modes of political subjectivity.

Viewed from the perspective of the state (which today places supreme emphasis on rational productivity), the riot amounts to a form of exceptional violence. Standing outside of and against the everyday, the riot is an interruption, an interjection. Through the riot, people emancipated themselves—however temporarily—from the norms of constituted power. By claiming, through their own actions, the power to declare the exception, rioters (regardless of whether or not it is their intent) challenge not only the particular policies or rules of the state, but the state itself. Through this process, the "everyday" status of the everyday world is itself called into question.

For, while the everyday world can be made to appear relatively free of violence through social and textual mediations, activists have long understood that this is not the case.[42] Because activism necessitates conflict with these very mediations, it provides a potential means of rematerializing the violence underlying the everyday world. And, when it takes the form of uproarious interjection, violence throws the tumult bubbling beneath the surface of our orderly republic into sharp relief. Through violence, it becomes clear that the everyday itself is a catastrophe.

As early as 1963, Betty Friedan was able to see the destitution writhing just below the surface of suburban perfection. The ordered, contained, and indisputably efficient world that the American dream had conjured into being simultaneously relied upon and effectively wrote out the desire to live from its equation. In place of life, women in Friedan's account were given survival—a mandate to be alive that was non-negotiable. According to Friedan, it was necessary to "understand how the very condition of being a housewife can create a sense of emptiness, non-existence, nothingness, in women." This is because "there are aspects of the housewife role that make it impossible for a woman of adult intelligence to retain a sense of human identity ... without which a human being, man or woman, is not truly alive" (1963: 305).

For housewives who could not live this way, the prescribed solution was found not in a change in circumstance but rather in a change of body. The suburb—the point at which the social reorganization of the American production-consumption matrix reaches its acme—demanded the housewife. And where "housewife" was untenable, it was made tenable through tranquilizers and other pharmaceutical interventions. There was no conspiracy. Everything was in plain view. And yet, as Friedan astutely pointed out, desperate women's experience remained "the problem with no name." As Giorgio Agamben suggested in reference to the Nazi concentration camp, we might say that the power at work in the suburbs remained "invisible in its very exposure, all the more hidden for showing itself as such" (156). For Friedan, the connection between suburban perfection and the experience of the Nazi concentration camp was explicit: "there is an uncanny, uncomfortable insight into why a woman can so easily lose her sense of self as a housewife in certain psychological observations made of the behavior of prisoners in Nazi concentration camps."

> In these settings, purposely contrived for the dehumanization of man, the prisoners literally became "walking corpses." Those who "adjusted" to the conditions of the camps surrendered their human identity and went almost indifferently to their deaths. Strangely enough, the conditions which destroyed the human identity of so many prisoners were not the torture and the brutality, but conditions similar to those which destroy the identity of the American housewife. (305–306)

Nowadays, *The Feminine Mystique* is more likely critiqued than read. Nevertheless, scattered throughout its pages, we find an excellent initial approximation of how an analysis of biopower might be extended to account for the experience of the American suburb. For Foucault, the advent of biopower helped to prompt the shift from Sovereign to state rule. This shift entailed a move away from the "deductive" mode of ruling (which claimed a "right to death" of any subject under regal sovereignty) toward an optimizing "power over life." According to Foucault, starting in the seventeenth century, "this power over life evolved in two basic forms."

> One of these poles ... centered on the body as a machine: its disciplining, the optimization of its capabilities, the extortion of its forces, the parallel increase of its usefulness and its docility, its integration into systems of efficient and economic controls, all this was ensured by the procedures of power that characterized the *disciplines*: an *anatomo-politics of the human body*. The second, formed somewhat later, focused on the species body, the body imbued with the mechanics of life and serving as the basis of the biological processes... Their supervision was effected through an entire series of interventions and *regulatory controls*: a *bio-politics of the population*. (1990: 139)

The ontological effects of these transformations are considerable. Biopower made an indelible mark on the human body and even called into question what it means to *be human*. And while idealist philosophy has been characterized by a long history of speculation on this very question, biopower emancipated these musings from the realm of abstraction and made them forebodingly concrete. "For millennia," Foucault noted, "man remained what he was for Aristotle: a living animal with the additional capacity for a political existence; modern man is an animal whose politics places his existence as a living being into question" (143).

In *Homo Sacer*, Agamben traces the philosophical and juridical elaboration of biopower to show how the Nazi concentration camp—far from being an unspeakable aberration—actually conformed (and stood as the perfect monument) to the logic of the modern world.[43] Central to this logic is the attribution of value to life. While the idealist impulse underlying modern experience made it possible for people to imagine *a life worth living*, the politicization of this sentiment pushed it toward its opposite. Fully realized, the politicization of life demanded an encounter with a threshold after which it became possible to envision *a life unworthy of being lived*. Strikingly, this eugenicist position emerged alongside conceptions of individual sovereignty. "It is as if every attribution of sovereignty and every 'politicization' of life (which, after all, is implicit in the sovereignty of the individual over his own existence)," argues Agamben, "necessarily implies a new decision concerning the threshold beyond which life ceases to be politically relevant, becomes only 'sacred,' life and can as such be eliminated without punishment."

> It is even possible that this limit, on which the politicization and the *exceptio* of natural life in the juridical order of the state depends, has done nothing but extend itself in the history of the West and has now—in the new biopolitical horizon of states with national sovereignty—moved inside every human life and every citizen. Bare life is no longer confined to a particular place or a definite category. It now dwells in the biological body of every living being. (139–140).

∎

The confrontation between the modern ideal of a life worth living and the frightening pronouncement of life "unworthy of being lived" finds dramatic literary expression in Chuck Palahniuk's *Fight Club*. Here, the accumulated perfection of the narrator's life—measured in units of furniture purchased from the IKEA catalogue—is pitted against the fleeting perfection that Tyler Durden, his alter ego, produces himself. In response to the despair of the everyday (traced along the fractured time zones of airplane departures and arrivals), the narrator seeks out life at rock bottom—the post-representational place where social mediations cease to register. And though it ends in an orgy of gunshot and explosives, *Fight Club*'s drama can't help but resonate with the more mundane experiences of the many activists who were inspired by it.[44] To get a sense of this appeal to the quotidian, it's useful to remember how, in the middle of Palahniuk's novel, Durden argues that getting fired "is the best thing that could happen to any of us. That way, we'd quit treading water and do something with our lives" (1996: 74).

The resonance is clear. The job from which we get fired is the opposite of "doing something"; real production (real politics) means doing something with "our lives"—with life itself; ontology passes through violence to become politics; at the moment we cease "treading water" and begin to engage in real production, we find the key to resolving the constitutive lack underlying human experience in the post-political era. In the context of the never-ending cycle of mundane existence, reconnecting with life beyond mediation is the ultimate seduction. It is for this reason that both the narrator and the reader identify with the messianic dimensions of Tyler Durden's excess.

These escapes from constraint are indeed enviable. Considered from the perspective of the problem of biopower, however, Durden's excesses are never fully realized (and can never be fully realized within the terms in which they are presented). Why? One compelling answer is this: because Durden's relationship with the narrator maps onto and reproduces the logic of modern biopower itself. As Agamben explains, "Biopower's supreme ambition is to produce, in the human body, the absolute separation of the living being and the speaking being, *zoë* and *bios*, the inhuman and the human" (156). The very power of the narrator (who both is and isn't Tyler Durden) to *narrate* Durden's vitalist excess rests on biopower's division of speaking and living.

The narrator tells Durden's story as a disciple honoring a fallen messiah. But despite the strong identification that activists sometimes developed with Durden's liberatory excesses, the ultimate impossibility of synthesizing Durden and the narrator into a single subject concedes the triumph of biopower. Durden had to be expelled. In the film, this is made explicit in the final scene where the narrator shoots himself and kills Durden. Now resolved through the bourgeois repression of living being, the narrator reenters the symbolic order and is able to assume his role in the heterosexual *telos* that unites him with his curious love interest, Marla Singer.

Although many activists were excited to see office towers destroyed, *Fight Club*'s conclusion is ultimately conservative because the contradiction yielded by the irreconcilability of the everyday does not become a catastrophe. Everything is resolved at the level of the signifier; the capacity for production does not become conscious of itself. Instead, it gets subsumed beneath an ethical gloss. The ethic it draws upon is that of non-violence—the preservation of what already exists. Although, as the narrator sheepishly admits, "you met me at a very strange time in my life," we are now set to get back to normal.

It's significant that the film is set up in such a way that, at the beginning, the viewer gravitates strongly toward Durden and his identification with living being while, by the end, the point of identification has shifted almost entirely over to the narrator. Durden, who eschews action at the level of the signifier ("sticking feathers up your butt does not make you a chicken"), allows the viewer to feel the seduction of living being. However, this seduction is meant to give way to dread the moment the viewer discovers the ethical costs of their identification. In the end, they are meant to feel grateful for the regulatory power of the narrator's speaking being. It is Aristotelian coercion, pure and simple.

This is how it works: Durden's *hamartia* (his lust for life, the source of both his triumph and his tragedy) brings on his *peripetia* (the point after which he must inevitably come undone). And the audience, having been gleefully seduced by the wonders of Durden's *hamartia*, ends by being grateful for the cathartic moment when—through the process of siding with its obverse—they are saved from their identification with what became the very source of the hero's downfall.[45] What this seemingly inevitable conclusion leaves out, however, is the possibility of a meaningful reunion of these two ontological fragments. In order for *Fight Club* to arrive at a radical conclusion, it would be necessary for Durden and the narrator to find a point of synthesis. Here, the objective is not to distance oneself from the wreckage of the past but to complete it.

■

In contrast to the narrow life stipend afforded by today's society of control, a genuine catastrophe presents itself as a magnificent opportunity (*Fight Club*'s narrator, who wishes for plane wrecks, knows this intuitively). It functions as both an interruption of the everyday and an injunction to make visible the depravity of the everyday itself. Whereas the everyday weaves lived experience into a seamless narrative of progress, catastrophe enables us to *begin*. In this way, identification with catastrophe enables us to wrest the promise of redemption from the failures of the past through a repetition that—*this time*—might yield a different outcome.

This was the hope underlying Walter Benjamin's *Theses on the Philosophy of History*—a document written just prior to his suicide prompted by the threat of Nazi deportation. According to Slavoj Žižek, the identification with the catastrophic failures and humiliations of the past in Benjamin's work "determines revolution as repetition which suspends linear historical progress: when a revolution conceives itself as a repetition of past failed revolutionary attempts, these attempts are rendered visible in their very 'openness.'" Because of this, "revolution 'delivers' the past failed attempts by repeating them in their possibility." Or, to put it another way: "it retroactively realizes their potentials which were crushed in the victorious course of 'official' history" (2008: 92).

The activist impulse to renounce identification with catastrophe on the basis of its immediate tactical efficacy is thus a grave mistake. By not making the breach caused by catastrophe the site of politics, activists effectively cede this ground to the society of control, which operates primarily by exploiting the impulse to live (indeed, it is solely by stimulating the will to live that the society of control is able to perpetuate itself through an unending cycle of substitution and deferral). One need only look to the aftermath of September

11 to see this process at work. Though people pulled together in the hours immediately following the attack, though strangers comforted one another on street corners in a fit of humanizing excess that violated every rule of New York propriety, the state quickly filled the gap.

Quickly lionized for his bravado in the aftermath of September 11, Rudy Giuliani came up with perhaps the most cynical formulation: returning to life as normal would be the best revenge. People were thus subdued, forced to retreat from the breach the catastrophe had created. And people who had managed to do much more than survive (who had found life beyond constraint in the brief moment when everything was up in the air) were instructed to return to their homes and jobs. And though homes and jobs may well signify the security for which people long, they are—statistically—far greater sites of ruin than Ground Zero.

To get a sense of the extent to which this is the case, it suffices to recall that, according to the United States Department of Labor, a total of 5,524 fatal work injuries were recorded in 2002—a number vastly outstripping the 2,976 estimated to have lost their lives in the World Trade Center. The number of casualties comes into still greater perspective when we consider that, according to the US Surgeon General, approximately 4,000 American women are beaten to death every year by the men with whom they live. However, because these deaths are—in a sense—part of the standard operating procedure of the neo-liberal world, it's easy for them to fall from view. They are predictable; they can be calculated. As such, they can be written off. In contrast, the catastrophe is open ended. No one knows what will happen next. And this is why, though its body count may seem modest when considered alongside the brutality of the everyday, it remains absolutely terrifying for those with a vested interest in the status quo.

■

Though its reach is never complete, the logical conclusion of the biopolitical project is the abolition of exteriority. By transposing the whole of the world into the representational register, today's society of control makes genuine (that is, transformative) production (that is, politics) impossible. By subordinating living being to speaking being, biopolitics produces a situation in which resistance in the first instance is necessarily "pre-political." Since the contemporary political field has been subsumed by representation (the logic of "action" at the level of the signifier), any attempt to connect to politics that does not first try to revitalize the capacities of living being will inevitably end by cannibalizing itself.

One of the principal means by which activists have sought to avoid representational cannibalization has been to intensify their connection to myths that stimulate the will to live. To be sure, in and of themselves, myths are highly ambivalent. Nevertheless, it's important to recognize the political significance of the activist desire to identify with figures that, like Durden, manage to elude the constraints of the everyday. Even when the content of those renegade lives seems repugnant, they nevertheless retain a kind of magnetic allure. Consider the resonance of a film like *Natural Born Killers*—a film that resonated with many activists[46] even though it provoked its audience to feel the very same "Mickey and Mallory fever" that it critiqued. Why did this film, which stimulated people's identification with living being only to submit them to the Aristotelian coercion of its conservative resolution, resonate so strongly?

Following Benjamin, we can say that it is because, at its most acute (and read from the standpoint of the constitutive lack underlying life without politics), the tabloid fascination with murderers is best understood as a mythic rehearsal of the drama of regicide. And though it may seem distant from our current political realities, we must concede that regicide remains the base unit, the underlying content, of all politics (it's not for nothing that, at the beginning of the second verse of *The Internationale*, the Communards asserted that the international working class needed "no condescending saviors / no gods, no Caesars, no tribune"). By usurping the rule of law, the murderer reveals more than the law's limited reach. By deciding what lives and what dies, murder uncovers the constitutive ground of sovereign power. In this way, the sovereignty of the state and the unanimity of deferral upon which it rests (the unanimity which Hobbes tried so mightily to enshrine in *Leviathan*) begin to appear precarious.

Even when this search for an outside does not yield its proper object, people tend not to be deterred in their search for that point at which sovereign power gives way to the possibility of a true production. In his "Critique of Violence," Benjamin drew the connection between violence, the mythic force of criminality, and the collective longing for exteriority in no uncertain terms:

> The law's interest in a monopoly of violence vis-à-vis individuals is not explained by the intention of preserving legal ends but, rather, by that of preserving the law itself; that violence, when not in the hands of the law, threatens it

not by the ends that it may pursue but by its mere existence outside the law. The same may be more dramatically suggested if one reflects how often the figure of the "great" criminal, however repellent his ends may have been, has aroused the secret admiration of the public. This cannot result from his deed, but only from the violence to which it bears witness. (1978: 281)

Activists have not been immune to this process of mythic identification. One need only to consider what transpired when *Rage Against The Machine* put Ché Guevera's face on a t-shirt to see the extent to which this is the case. And while it's fashionable to critique this kind of hero-worship (by claiming, for instance, that the commodity form robs such an identification of its critical potential, or that the lives lived by those who sported his image have little in common with Ché's guerrilla escapades, or that many *Rage* fans had little or no idea about who Ché was or what he stood for, etc. etc.), the t-shirt nevertheless signaled an identification with a *potential* that was, by definition, outside of the bounds of the gated community.

Consequently, activists would do well to recognize the tremendous energy contained in the longing this identification entails. And while it remains a distorted manifestation of the inexpressible desire to *really live*, we shouldn't pretend that it could be otherwise; in the first instance, desire *always* assumes the form of some already-existent thing. Many activists who, during the period of anti-globalization struggles, moved in the direction of riotous excess undoubtedly have a *Rage Against the Machine* t-shirt buried somewhere in their closet. And though it might be satisfying, the "not radical enough" critique amounts more to snobbery than to a real understanding of the process at work.

At its worst, it subordinates the whole question of radical politics to the representational register. Here, *Rage* and Ché are replaced by some more worthy signifier of resistance (say, Sacco and Vanzetti). In response to this tendency, it's necessary to recognize that—in the first instance—the content of mythic identifications is less important than the orientation to the promise of exteriority that such identifications encourage. By reconnecting people immersed in the representational domain to the feelings of lack that mark their expulsion from politics, myth stimulates the desire to pass through violence in order to reconnect to politics.

In contexts where the mythic figure has attained its status by virtue of an ability to escape the constraints of representational politics, identification with this mythic figure demands a productive extension of the Self into unknown territory. As Ernst Bloch put it, "it has fallen to the criminals to feel fear, remorse, guilt, the stirring of the germ of the spirit in us." For those who would not follow, Bloch surmises that their "hearts" must "stay lethargic" (2000: 166). The power of myth is precisely that it produces the condition for subjects to act beyond the constraints of their everyday realities in order to produce new truths. In this way, myth paradoxically reveals itself to be truth's precondition.

■

Recounting the fascination with the general strike that pervaded the French working class at the beginning of the twentieth century, Georges Sorel came to similar conclusions. According to Sorel, engagement with myths—especially those that are held in common—needn't condemn believers to narcissistic delusion or to a disavowal of reality. Instead, by enabling actions that exceed the bounds of what already exists, myth compels its adherents to strive toward the resolution of the contradictions underlying reality itself. Although Sorel's focus on the general strike might seem detached from today's meager possibilities, the methodological impulse underlying his investigation remains profoundly applicable. "Without leaving the present, without reasoning about [the] future, which seems forever condemned to escape our reason," Sorel suggested, "we would be unable to act at all."

> Experience shows that *the framing of a future, in some indeterminate time*, may, when it is done in a certain way, be very effective, and have very few inconveniences; this happens when the anticipation of the future takes the form of those myths, which enclose with them, all the strongest inclinations of a people … inclinations which recur to the mind with the insistence of instincts in all the circumstances of life; and which give an aspect of complete reality to all the hopes of the immediate action by which, more easily than by any other method, men can reform their desires, passions and mental activity. We know, furthermore, that these social myths in no way prevent a man from profiting by the observations which he makes in the course of his life, and form no obstacle to the pursuit of his normal occupations. (2004: 124–125)

The danger with myths is that they may compel people to cast themselves into passive roles. They can become consolation prizes, narcotizing agents in a pharmacy of regulatory catharsis (indeed, this is the role they play in the capitalist marketplace where they stimulate the desire to consume). But like any compound in the *pharmakon*, the myth has the potential to be both medicine and poison. It's therefore crucial that "the framing of a future" be done, as Sorel says, "in a certain way." Since it arises from "all the strongest inclinations of a people," Sorel's general strike avoids the pitfall of poison and passivity. It's therefore necessary to ask: what, in today's biopolitical universe inhabited by white middle class dissidents, might stand as a counterpart to this myth? Although it's now a decade old, I maintain that the Battle of Seattle and the Black Bloc actions that took place there remain one of the most likely candidates for elevation to this status.

For, while Seattle can be understood as the practical outcome of practical considerations, its mythic dimensions are indebted to the event's disclosure of an unrealized future. This future permeated the event; it demanded that those present become fully invested in the consequentiality of their actions. Whatever the practical limitations of the movement's campaign on N30, the recognition of potential (in the sense both of power and possibility) gave the event mythic force. This force managed to spread well beyond the sleepy northwest. For a brief moment, it managed to infect countless nodes in the world system. And though the waters have receded, the mark they left when they reached their high point is both taunting and inspiring. For those who recognize that historical change requires that we honor our debts to the past, the non-resolution of Seattle's promise only heightens its significance.

Activists have expressed an understandable desire to not get tied down by Seattle (or, more generally, by the whole paradigm of anti-globalization struggles). Nevertheless, the profoundly ecstatic character of the event has made it difficult to forget. To get a sense of this rupture, it's useful to remember how *shocking* it was to read the words "we are winning" spray-painted on a wall in the middle of the Seattle tumult. Activists frequently claim small victories to console themselves; however, the fact that *this* proclamation corresponded so directly to the situation infused it with mythic significance. Is it any wonder, then, that the Turbulence Collective returned to this image as they assessed the possibility of revitalizing the best aspects of the anti-globalization movement in the lead up to the 2007 G8 meeting in Germany?

Despite the need to look forward, we must recognize the ongoing value of Seattle as a reference point. This value arises principally from the fundamentally unresolved character of the event itself—from the fact that the promise it entailed has yet to be realized. The components of the myth (that people can work together across difference, that the state's might is nothing when compared to the strength of dissident refusal, that catastrophe and solidarity share a profound co-implication) continue to reveal their lasting truth.

Most criticisms of the anti-globalization movement aimed at the chasm that separated the myth from the reality that unfolded. However, the resolution of the movement's failures can't be found in the disavowal of the myth. Just the opposite: myth becomes the means by which people can orient to the event's promise in order to complete it. Past and future conspire in a time called *now*. It's a moment that arises from the decisive action of the dissident herself.

The time of the now is not upon us. We're still in the endless present. With the first cycle of anti-globalization struggle over but with the character and scale of the second one not yet determined, many activists—especially those coming from the white middle class—have confronted a demobilizing wall of uncertainty. And they have good reason: modern life gives us countless reasons to despair. Under conditions like these, we would be well within our right to kill ourselves. But when we decide not to, when we pass through violence in order to discover the life that lies beyond it, we enter into an agreement in which our actions become the sole measure of our being. According to Sartre, such moments enable profound ontological transformation. They also require that people go beyond themselves in order to avoid succumbing: "If nothing compels me to save my life, nothing prevents me from precipitating myself into the abyss. The decisive conduct will emanate from a self which I am not yet" (69). It's hard to be in two places at once. But, some might add, it's even harder to remain trapped in the interminable present.

For today's white middle class, there are only two choices: death or life. Killing oneself and not choosing amount to the same thing. The only remaining path is to assume responsibility for everything. It's the only resolution to the melancholic lack underwriting today's society of control. However, the decision to assume responsibility for everything is not yet awareness of what "everything" entails. Only by passing through violence and entering the field of politics do we come to see the world in its totality; only then do we begin to perceive the full scope of the potential for transformation.

In 1957, Albert Camus told an interviewer that, "since atomic war would divest any future of its meaning, it gives us complete freedom of action. We have nothing to lose except everything. This is the wage of our generation" (1995: 247). Though activists in the global north may yet die under a hail of bombs, it's more likely that the "wage of our generation" will emerge not from the threat of annihilation but rather from the deranged logic of unending optimization. In order to muster a refusal, in order to embody resistance and assume the responsibility implied by "complete freedom of action," white middle class dissidents must first pass collectively, in a riot of our own, through violence in order to enter the realm of politics. The Black Bloc marked the threshold between our world and the one we need to create. By flirting with the limit situation, they showed us the way.

·REPRESENTATION'S LIMIT

Positing a conceptual identity between activism and terrorism has not customarily been a project of the Left. Exactly the opposite seems to be true. Since the nineteenth century, the history of political repression reads in part as a story of precisely this opportunistic conflation. Invoking the spectre of terrorism has been one of the means by which social movement actors have been excluded from the realm of legitimate claim making. Today, the expansive conception of "enemy" underwriting America's war on terror—now focused increasingly on the domestic threat of eco-activists—confirms the relative ease, pervasiveness, and longevity of this conflation. Given the grave consequences of being labeled a terrorist, it's not surprising that activists have worked hard to distance themselves from the category. Because of terrorism's inevitable exclusion from the law, and given the extent to which social movements have relied upon the relative stability of rights to make political claims,[47] the activist denunciation of terrorism makes complete sense.

However, despite activist claims to the contrary, history reveals that both social movement action and terrorism share a common provenance. In their modern forms, both social movements and terrorism arose in the late eighteenth century and came into their own during the nineteenth century. Both were made possible by the contradictory dynamics of the bourgeois public sphere. Both are the bastard children of a political world the bourgeoisie created in its own image. That world was shaped first and foremost by the problem of representation. During the nineteenth century, because "the public" was viewed as a political object that was not yet a for-itself political actor, the trick was to relate to it in a manner that would compel it to yield desired outcomes.

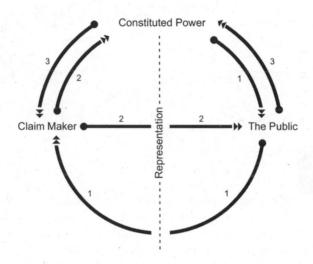

In this arrangement, wherein political claim-makers arise from the public and conceptually distinguish themselves from it, a threefold process arises: The public is subject to the whims of constituted power and passes this experience on to the claim-makers that arise from within its midst but who are conceptually distinct from them. The claim-makers then act upon constituted power and, by passing through the film of representation, upon the public as well. Once acted upon in this fashion, the public sometimes responds by reversing the cyclic dynamic of the process in order to act upon constituted power. For its part, constituted power sometimes acts on the claim maker at this point.[48]

The public sphere was necessary for the consolidation of bourgeois rule. It enabled the bourgeoisie to displace the feudal aristocracy. However, the necessary inclusion—even if only nominal—of "the public" meant that bourgeois rule was marked by a conflict between their political means and their mode of political development. Social movements—and socialism itself—crawled into the world through this breach.

However, unlike socialism (which, by virtue of its emphasis on production, began to develop a post-representational conception of dual power), social movements became contentious actors *within* the representational paradigm of the bourgeois public sphere (cf. Tilly 2004: 138). Whether or not it was their intention (although often it was), social movements encouraged people to identify with the bourgeoisie's legitimating structures. Or, to put it another way, social movements legitimated the "is" of the public sphere by demanding that it live up to the promise of its "ought." Although their methods were different, terrorists gravitated toward this same point of ambiguity.

Recounting the actions of Auguste Vaillant, an anarcho-terrorist who threw a bomb in the French National Assembly in 1893 and said "the more they are deaf, the more your voice must thunder out so that they will understand you," Alex P. Schmid and Janny de Graaf explain how "the unequal chances of expressing oneself, brought about by the rise of the big press, contributed to the rise of terrorism as 'expressive' politics" (1982: 11). Both social movements and terrorists sought to affect the public by launching assaults on constituted power in order to intervene in political processes to which they had no direct access. Both perceived the public in representational terms.

Initially, both social movements and terrorists were able to produce significant effects within the bourgeois public sphere. Perhaps one of the most significant victories (and one of the points at which social movements and terrorism most fully overlapped) came from the struggle for women's suffrage. However, the suffragettes' move away from representational to spectacular violence corresponded to a shift in the optimism that movements felt about the opportunities afforded by the public sphere. As that sphere began to narrow through the course of the twentieth century, both social movements and terrorism became estranged from the public.

This situation produced an impasse. Having accepted the public sphere as their terrain of struggle, and having acclimatized to its later spectacularization, both social movements and terrorists—despite their radical programs—became ensnared in the representational machinery of bourgeois politics. Although they contested the content of bourgeois rule (and although they critiqued the moribund character of the representational apparatus), they nevertheless started by taking the bourgeois commitment to representational politics as self-evident.

By refusing to identify the significant continuities between the activist and terrorist orientation to the representational politics of spectacular capitalism (by failing to consider the continuity between activist and terrorist orientations to "the public"), social movements have forfeited the possibility of engaging in a form of auto-criticism that could significantly enhance the consequences of our political activity.

The proposition that activists should turn their critique of terrorism into an auto-critique should not be understood as an attack on the occasional use of violent tactics to which movements have sometimes felt entitled. Just the opposite: the critique of social movement allegiances to bourgeois representational "politics" enables activists to engage *more completely and more productively* in forms of political violence. The critique of terrorism as bastard inversion of bourgeois representational "politics," when extended as auto-critique, enables us to begin envisioning our violence in the "pure" or productive form considered by Walter Benjamin in 1921. Paradoxically, contemporary activists are closer to terrorists when we choose to make our interventions in the register of the spectacular rather than engaging directly in productive violence.

■

In *Refractions of Violence* (2003), Martin Jay recounts how the shipwreck can serve as the marker of epistemological moments. In ancient Greece, the shipwreck stood—for the witness, at least—as the mark of Nature's irrefutability. Being torn apart at sea was a sober reminder of the relationship between man and his world. Later, for thinkers like Pascal, the shipwreck would provide the witness with a smug satisfaction. Good judgment and sure footing on dry land, Pascal intoned, would save some while others drowned. By the time of Nietzsche, all dry land had vanished. Cast adrift and lacking even a moral compass, the best one could do was to keep from being subsumed. The spectator and the shipwreck began to share an eerie proximity.

By the beginning of the twentieth century, the spectator celebrated (or was forced to deal with) sensorial immediacy as a regular feature of everyday life. At the World's Fairs, people were treated to the possibility of riding whirling contraptions that, in some instances, were meant to replicate the feeling of being seasick. Once the precondition for moral reflection, the mediated standpoint of the spectator had been totally supplanted by unadulterated presence. It is a state that shows no sign of abating. In hindsight, the story of the twentieth century may well be told as a story about the intensification of the simultaneous experiences of proximate distance and distant proximity. It was precisely this phenomenon that Guy Debord described in his *Society of the Spectacle*.

For Debord, even though the images that pervaded spectacular society ostensibly continued to represent the things they signified, the spectacle itself made it increasingly difficult for the viewer to reconnect the image of the thing to the thing itself. What was true in Debord's time is even truer today; representation—as formalized in bourgeois epistemology—makes it difficult for people to experience themselves as participants in the world of the signified. Consequently, the signifier (the image emancipated from its referent) becomes everything. Unmediated experience, like the fear and trembling that the ancient Greeks felt before the shipwreck, begins to recede into a mythological past.

How can radicals work to heal the divide between signifier, representation, and consumption, on the one hand, and the signified, the real, and production on the other? Since the advent of the bourgeois public sphere (and especially since its mid-twentieth century spectacular transformation), political violence has often been marshaled to produce effects at the level of the signifier. However, violence as such corresponds more directly to the sphere of production and to activity at the level of the signified. Its attributes correspond to the attributes of the labor process outlined by Marx in Chapter VII of *Capital*. Reconnecting with violence as a productive act (an act where production happens directly and not by way of mediating proxy forces) will allow social movements to move away from terrorism and enable them to begin pushing against the representational limits of the bourgeois horizon.

■

In May 1968, students and workers took to the streets of Paris and nearly sparked a revolution. Among their other remarkable slogans was the wisdom "*sous les pavés, la plage.*" The point was simple, beautiful, and concrete. Underneath these cobblestones was sand. Underneath the order that constituted power has imposed was a world of unstructured time, a world of possibility. With every cobblestone ripped from the street and hurled at the CRS, demonstrators would come one step closer to uncovering what was possible. What was hidden would be revealed. The force of action would bring into view all that had been buried.

In April of 2005, a demonstration and street party called *Karna[ge]val* also took to the streets of Paris. These demonstrators also aimed to uncover what was hidden. The *double entendre* of the party's name made clear what was at stake. The carnivalesque world of the spectacle had bracketed within it a moment of destruction. This bracketed ruin would be illuminated, however, by the carnival the demonstrators would unleash to confront it. And so, while the balance of the visible and the hidden had been flipped (in 1968, beauty needed to be uncovered; at *Karna[ge]val* beauty itself was the mask behind which carnage hid), the project appeared to be the same.

As I arrived at Place de la République on the afternoon of April 9, I was confronted with the beautiful site of thousands of people—mostly young and mostly crusty—taking over the park in the middle of the square. Circled around the edge of the park were dozens of vans rigged up with sound systems playing deep house music. The gathering stood out like a sore thumb in the middle of an otherwise well-behaved neighborhood. From the adjacent sidewalks, onlookers gathered to gawk or shake their heads in dismay. As I got closer to the center of the action, someone handed me a leaflet.

> *Encore une fois nous devons reprendre le pavé pour une manifestation revendifestive, afin d'affirmer nos convictions artistiques et culturelles, de revendiquer clairement notre volonté de nous démarquer des logiques de consommation et de soumission aux ordres du marché, notre refus des dérives sécuritaires et démagogiques subies par notre société. Mettons en lumière le rôle créatif et social des groupes informels d'activistes, des sound-systems, des pratiques culturelles amateurs, des secteurs émergents bref, de tous ceux grâce à qui le mot culture ne se résume pas à quelques grandes institutions ou industries produisant de grands spectacles destinés à des consommateurs-clients...*

"Once again, we must reclaim the streets to demonstrate and affirm our artistic and cultural convictions..." The action was aimed squarely at the depravity of market relationships and the opulence of consumption. In opposition to this paradigm, which the organizers claimed required both "demagogy" and a creeping "securitization" of the public sphere, the activists gathered on that day spoke instead of the creativity flourishing outside (or beneath) the market. Here, the leaflet explained, people were producing without a thought for the spectacle and its endless supply of consumer clients.

Although it was not yet the festival of the oppressed promised by Marx, the gathering was nevertheless a striking counterpoint to the neighborhood in which it had assembled. Hundreds of kids gathered around sound systems and danced wildly in the middle of the street. Others climbed the austere statues in the middle of the park and, like spiders, began spinning colored ribbon in the wind. Below them on the grass, activists gathered in small and large groups and passed around bottles of beer and wine. Although the CRS could be seen at every corner of the square, they kept their distance.

Lacking a clear message or explicit goal beyond self-expression in the context of its general prohibition, *Karna[ge]val* encouraged people to create an alternative space within the constraints of the everyday. Although event organizers negotiated a parade route with the police, the gathering did not feel contrived. As an unruly presence within an otherwise tranquil neighborhood, it enabled a brief disruption in the immediate flow of what Debord had called the "common stream in which the unity of this life can no longer be reestablished" (1983: 2). In this respect, *Karna[ge]val* exceeded the permits it had been granted.

But despite the possibility of energetic spillover, activists on the march made little effort to engage with the people on the event's sidelines. Maybe the organizers and participants simply sought to create an alternative space in which to enjoy the initial approximations of a new kind of community. But if community was all that was sought, then the point of staging the action at Place de la République is not entirely obvious. Certainly, feelings of solidarity could just as easily have arisen in the darkened warehouses of the dance scene—spaces that had furnished the vast majority of participants for the day's action. What did the disapproving gaze of the mainstream bring to this event that would not have been there otherwise?

In a kind of double move, where one invites the gaze of the public while simultaneously refusing to acknowledge it, the object of this demonstration became the participants' refusal itself. Whatever the disruption to the immediate flow in the common stream in which the unity of life can no longer be reestablished, there remained a more important assertion of ontological distance. *Karna[ge]val* was an exercise in negating the bourgeois representational order. By trying to arrest the flow of the modern spectacle's imperceptible immediacy, *Karna[ge]val* stood as a potentially important pedagogical opportunity. However, to the extent that its critique of the spectacle became spectacular (to the extent that it operated not at the level of the signified but rather at the level of the signifier), it's doubtful that those pedagogical opportunities could ever be fulfilled.

■

In *The Spirit of Terrorism*, Jean Baudrillard advanced a now-familiar argument about the importance of images. Rehearsing positions established in his earlier

work, Baudrillard argued that *the visual* had become central to the experience
of terrorism. What remains in the aftermath of the attack are the images. The
very experience of September 11, Baudrillard claimed, was *the same as* "the
sight of the images."

> This impact of the images, and their fascination, are necessarily what we
> retail, since images are, whether we like it or not, our primal scene. And
> at the same time as they have radicalised the world situation, the events in
> New York can also be said to have radicalised the relation of the image to
> reality. Whereas we were dealing before with an uninterrupted profusion of
> banal images and a seamless flow of sham events, the terrorist act in New
> York has resuscitated both images and events. (27)

Baudrillard's assessment says as much about the spectacular state of the
present as it does about terrorism. Indeed, the "uninterrupted profusion of
banal images and [the] seamless flow of sham events" seems to be derived from
the same list of concerns that motivated Debord. However, for Baudrillard,
it is in the terrorist act—and not "the situation"—that the power to rupture
our cycle of endless repetitions is located. It is terrorism that elevates image and event to a new status. It is terrorism that brings image and event
closer together. The disjuncture between signifier and signified is resolved in
catastrophe.

Two accounts of epistemic and political resolution seem to be at work
here. In the first, image and event come together and things and their names
once again become inseperable. In the second, image and event come together
because the image—through its expansive mutations—consumes the event
entirely. It becomes its representational proxy (the copy for which there is no
original, Baudrillard's simulacrum). The experience of shock brought about
by terrorism seems to promise the former resolution. In fact, it delivers the
latter. However, because the latter (by its very logic) becomes all, it absorbs the
former as a trace, a spectral possibility. In reality, there are not two strategies.
There are only two phases of a single process by which the image is reener-
gized as a modality of representational politics. And so, while the *content* of
people's experience is transformed by representational catastrophe, their *mode*
of experiencing is not.

The fact that this disruption can feel radical arises not from an epistemological break but a political one, where a short circuit in the representational
sequence causes it to momentarily come undone. However, while the terrorist

act suggests that the terrorist is engaged in what Benjamin described as law-making violence, the act nevertheless remains bound by the representational logic of bourgeois epistemology. It's an action in excess of the law that serves in the end to reaffirm the law itself. The sovereign claim-maker who does not (and cannot) attain to sovereignty itself ends by being "enemy" and, in this fashion, provides the basis for the revitalization of constituted power. Consequently, Debord felt that the state itself invented terrorism as its representational negation, the enemy other that confirms it (1990). The same can be said, on a different level, of contemporary state responses to social movements.[49]

Under late capitalism, the image is perceived not as distinct from—but rather as constitutive of—reality. Since this is the case, the interjection of the spectacular act will tend not to reconcile image and reality but rather to confirm (or further enable) the process of "resolution" whereby the image consumes reality itself. In this way, it reestablishes a kind of proxy form of epistemological unity. For Baudrillard, the experience of sensorial immediacy that overcomes a viewer considering an action movie appears to be the only remaining register of experience in a world where the liar has lied to himself.

In a world where action at the level of the signified is perceived to be the stuff of religion, the expert manipulation of the signifier becomes the sole stuff of politics. To the extent that those who planned the attacks on the World Trade Center spoke in a language their targets would understand (killing people without cameras would not have done the trick), they rearticulated the epistemological conventions of bourgeois "politics" in its spectacular-representational moment. In this moment, production is subordinated to consumption and the signifier becomes indistinguishable from the thing itself.

■

How do we account for the persistence of representation and its enduring role as epistemological substructure to bourgeois politics? How do we account for the fact that, even when shaken by events that brought the reality of the image to bear in all its visceral presence, representation (a concept that carries within it the spectral trace of the signified and, as such, is susceptible to immanent critique) has endured as the primary mode of political engagement? In order to answer these questions, it's useful to consider the location of the terrorist act within the realm of experience. Specifically, it's useful to delineate the way that terrorist acts intersect with and respond to the configuration of the public sphere in the period of late capitalism. Here, terrorism comes into view as a strategy aimed at disrupting the continuity of the exchange between *the mass* and *the passerby*.

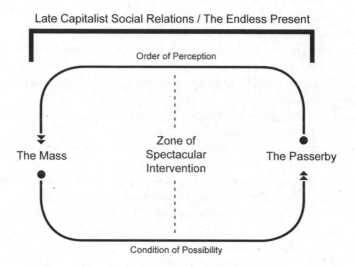

Referring to the diagram, we can see how *the mass* is bound within the field of the social. As a result of the dissimulations of late capitalism, the social itself is only perceptible through distorted and once-removed traces. *The mass* is one such perceptual effect. It's a representational achievement of its individual member, who distinguishes herself from the object of her contemplation by assuming the position of *the passerby*. In this arrangement, *the mass* (not yet rendered as such) is the condition of possibility for *the passerby*. At the same time, *the mass* as such only emerges through its recognition by *the passerby* herself. Even though it confronts *the passerby* as a coherent entity, *the mass* is in fact a perceptual object generated through contemplation.[50]

The position of *the passerby* is a serial category denoting an epistemological habit by which the world is rendered representationally intelligible through contemplation. As such, the position of *the passerby* is generic and can be occupied by any single person within *the mass*. Consequently, the *passerby*—despite being enamored with the experience of individuality enabled by their contemplative standpoint—can never escape the responsibility of playing a component part of *the mass* for the other.

Embodying the spectral qualities of market relations, *the mass* is the base unit of late capitalist experience. Here, people are assembled on the basis of consumption, and in relation to market arrangements. With the advent of late capitalism, *the mass* itself begins to take on the attributes of a commodity in the market. Although, by virtue of their practical activity, people are part of this *mass*, they only dimly perceive themselves in the object itself. Describing this relationship, Debord wrote: "in the spectacle, one part of the world represents itself to the world and is superior to it."

> The spectacle is nothing more than the common language of this separation. What binds the spectators together is no more than the irreversible relation at the very center which maintains their isolation. The spectacle reunites the separate, but reunites it *as separate*. (29)

Here, what binds spectators together is their mutual imbrication in a social relation that cannot be reversed. This is rendered concretely in the diagram above where *the mass* is the condition of possibility for *the passerby* but also an effect of *the passerby*'s recognition. The social connection between Debord's individuated spectators (who are equivalents to *the passerby* in the diagram) is achieved through their mutual but atomized relationship to *the mass* of which they all constitute a part for the other. The social, which is rendered invisible by this never-ending circuit of representation and recognition, corresponds to a signified that—from the standpoint of perception—can no longer be named directly. This perceptual occlusion arises from the very structure of capitalist social relations.

By simultaneously inviting the gaze and refusing to acknowledge it, the terrorist manages to momentarily disrupt the *mass–passerby* circuit. Nevertheless, the circuit's condition of possibility—its material substratum—remains untouched. Without a decisive challenge to bourgeois epistemology, even the seemingly pure act—violence as an end in itself—can be recuperated as image. And while the intensified image heightens the experience of presence for the viewer, this presence is not yet direct engagement with the material world. For that, another kind of violence is required.

We thus find, in the attack on the World Trade Center, an intensification of the basic epistemological move underlying *Karna[ge]val*. The bastard children of the public sphere know how to torment their parents; what they can't yet do is assume the responsibility of bringing to birth a new world from the ashes of the old. In the end, despite the severity of their respective tantrums, the actions of both activists and terrorists conform to the bourgeois politics of demand ("recognize us") even as they deny the necessary allegiance to consti-tuted power that such a demand entails.

■

What emerges from the momentary short-circuiting of the representational cycle brought about by activist and terrorist acts is an open question. On the one hand, the rupture can take the shape of an illumination, a moment when all the contingent activity that makes up the social world comes into view (a moment where crisis reveals the underlying ordering of social relations and the precariousness of their assembly). This is undoubtedly what activists hope for when they set out to break the spell of the spectacle. The new situation, although it emerges through spectacular means, is meant to demonstrate that there are never really spectators, only participants.

On the other hand, the rupture in the representational circuit can lead to a break with certainty that produces not illumination but atomization. To be sure, people's experiences under late capitalism are already highly individu-ated. Nevertheless, the representational *mass* operates as proxy for prior forms of collectivity for which people still long. The abolition of *the mass* achieved by overloading the representational circuit momentarily deprives people of this index. Caught in the representational field without any intelligible refer-ence point, *the passerby* retreats from the social. This outcome is of little use to activists.

If forms of representational action, no matter how critical (or how violent), have a tendency to reiterate the epistemological premises of the bourgeois world, what should activists do? How do we overcome the limits of the bour-geois horizon? One option is to cease conceiving our movements as claim-making agencies and to begin seeing them as modes of production instead. In order get our bearings while contemplating this transition, it's useful to revisit the lessons conveyed in Walter Benjamin's essay on violence.

Describing the emergence of the modern spectacular realm of parlia-mentary politics, Benjamin noted how "when the consciousness of the latent presence of violence in a legal institution disappears, the institution falls into decay. In our times, parliaments provide an example of this. They offer the familiar, woeful spectacle because they have not remained conscious of the revolutionary force to which they owe their existence" (1978: 288). Which is to say: to the extent that it remains sovereign, parliamentarianism rests not on law-making but rather on law-preserving violence. This kind of violence is managerial rather than productive. It commits people to custodial care for the existing world. In contrast to law-preserving violence, law-making violence entails a production, a contest between competing sovereign agencies. However, because the new reality is itself transposed *post festum* into law, it once again becomes representationally distorted.

Benjamin contrasts these forms of violence to what he calls divine violence. This violence is both productive and post-representational. It does not cede to law and is the preserve of neither activism nor terrorism. Its provenance is not the bourgeois public sphere. Its mode is not spectacular intervention. It does not seek to transform the meaning of the perceptually consumed object. Its vocation is an unending production that, at its threshold, yields an absolute reconciliation of subject and object.

This kind of violence is not available to anyone in the first instance. In order to acquire it, activists must renounce their parents and leave the house of representational politics. Because it necessarily entails the forfeiture of the state-granted rights upon which activism currently depends, it requires the willingness to assume all the duties and obligations of a usurper. But even by orienting *analytically* toward this kind of violence, activists could begin to draw a clear distinction between themselves and the representational sphere.

Since activists operating under current conditions in Canada and the US are not yet able to assume the responsibilities of the usurper (and since the forms of political activity in which we are currently engaged seem destined to infuse the representational cycle with a new vitality), it's necessary to consider practical first steps in the direction of divine violence.

Provisionally, it's worth contemplating what might be gained from a new asceticism of the act. What kind of unbearable energy might accumulate if we did not rely upon the cathartic resolution of representational action? If, instead of blowing off steam, violence was presented as an analytic device, as a means of breaking the posited identity between a concept and the thing it represents (if violence was mobilized not in the interest of a physical but rather an intellectual confrontation with the bourgeois world), then it's possible that those of us engaged in activist struggles could—in some indeterminate future—envision forms of engagement that could transform activism from a mode of representation into a mode of production.

In this way, activists could transform themselves as well. We will know the decisive moment has come when we cease to be followers of causes and become producers of effects instead.

NOTES

Introduction

1   In 1926, Gramsci asked: "How many times have I wondered if it is really possible to forge links with a mass of people when one has never had strong feelings for anyone, not even one's own parents; if it is possible to have a collectivity when one has not been deeply loved oneself by individual human creatures. Hasn't this had some effect on my life as a militant—has it not tended to make me sterile and reduce my quality as a revolutionary by making everything a matter of pure intellect, of pure mathematical calculation?"

2   As James Baldwin recounts with respect to white people in *The Fire Next Time*, "The person who distrusts himself has no touchstone for reality—for this touchstone can be only oneself. Such a person interposes between himself and reality nothing less than a labyrinth of attitudes. And these attitudes, furthermore, though the person is usually unaware of it (is unaware of so much!), are historical and public attitudes" (1964: 57).

3   And here it is useful to remember that "utopia" literally means "no place." As I will make clear, this fantasy (which arises from and is made possible through a disavowal of material grounding) is for the white middle class simultaneously a site of great opportunity and great fear.

4   For a good breakdown of the techniques of power brought about in the moment of governmentality, including the audit, insurance, training, and security, see Nikolas Rose's (1999) *Powers of Freedom: Reframing Political Thought*.

5   http://www.cwsworkshop.org/workshops/argj.html

6   In their *Terrorism 2002–2005* report, the FBI found that 22 of the 24 recorded "terrorist incidents" from 2002 to 2005 were allegedly perpetrated by "special interest extremists active in the animal rights and environmental movements." Many of these activists were subsequently rounded up in the "green scare." Their political sensibilities often emerged through engagement with the anti-globalization movement. For more on the green scare, see Monagham and Walby (2008).

7   For readers of Walter Benjamin, this approach will be instantly familiar. As Benjamin noted to himself in Convolute N of *The Arcades Project*, "it is not the economic origins of culture that will be presented, but the expression of the economy in its culture. At issue, in other words, is the attempt to grasp an economic process as perceptible *Ur*phenomenon" (2003: 460).

8   On this point, Shulamith Firestone remains exemplary in her fearless assertion of what most people remain too squeamish to admit: "Pregnancy is the temporary deformation of the body of the individual for the sake of the species" (1970: 180). The violence of the situation is undeniable. However, as Firestone notes, this violence has been dramatically concealed by the "School of the Great Experience," which allows people to indulge in the perverse pleasure of conceiving what's necessary as though it were chosen freely.

9   To cite but one example, Michael Barnholden (2005) summarizes how, during the early twentieth century, white workers in Vancouver effectively strengthened the position of white capitalists by rioting against Chinese and Japanese workers and businesses. By keeping these groups in check through extra-legal means, white workers effectively sided with their employers. Although some of these riots were marked by anti-capitalist sentiments, the racist distortion (the resolution of the problem at the level of representation) meant that these sentiments were ultimately harnessed to purposes at odds with working class interests.

One: Semiotic Street Fights

10   The November 30, 1999 demonstrations against the World Trade Organization's Millennial Round meetings in Seattle were, for many, the starting point of the anti-globalization movement. Although the demonstration was larger than anything many had seen up until that point, its significance was to be found elsewhere. By physically blocking delegates from accessing the meeting and by engaging in limited forms of property destruction, activists managed, in some small fashion, to shift the definition of "protest" itself

11 The April 21, 2001 demonstrations against the Free Trade Area of the Americas meetings in Quebec City represented the high point of anti-globalization activism on this side of the Atlantic. During these demonstrations, several thousand activists challenged and occasionally succeeded in tearing down an enormous security perimeter fence. Throughout the demonstration, police—numbering in the thousands—fired more than 5000 tear gas canisters at demonstrators. Quebec City is also significant in that it represents the first major attempt by anti-globalization activists in Canada and the US to organize a mass action along openly anti-capitalist lines.

12 Hansard: 1st Session, 37th Parliament, Vol 139, Iss. 27. Tuesday, April 24, 2001.

13 http://www.zmag.org/ZMag/articles/sept01starhawk.htm

14 Perhaps the greatest historical example of this exhortation can be found in Leon Trotsky's attack on the hypocrisy of bourgeois moralists (represented with ambassadorial fanfare by John Dewey) in his work *Their Morals and Ours* (1973).

15 Foucault reminds us of the significance of the word "monster" when, in *Madness and Civilization*, he points to its etymology. "The Monster" is literally something in need of being shown (1988, 70).

16 Demonstrators demanded that the province reverse a 20% welfare cut, reintroduce the landlord-tenant act (replaced by the egregiously named "tenant protection act"), and put an end to "community action policing"—a form of targeted policing that systematically intimidated and bullied the poor, the homeless, and people of color.

17 The fear of anthrax poisoning that gripped the United States in the months following September 11, for instance, recast the gas mask as a kind of security blanket. For a brief period of time, gas masks were as American as apple pie.

18 Jackson's report was prompted by demonstrations against the World Petroleum Congress taking place in Calgary that summer.

19 The Keeper is a reusable menstrual cup noted for its economic and environmental benefits, its demystification of menstrual blood, and its role in the prevention of toxic shock syndrome associated with tampons.

Three: Bringing the War Home
20   "Where Was the Color in Seattle?: Looking for reasons why the Great Battle was so white" by Elizabeth Martinez (*Colorlines*: Volume 3, Number 1, Spring 2000). All citations from this article have been taken from the online version found at http: //www.colours.mahost.org/articles/martinez.html

21   The PGA hallmarks emphasize: 1) A very clear rejection of capitalism, imperialism and feudalism; all trade agreements, institutions and governments that promote destructive globalisation; 2) We reject all forms and systems of domination and discrimination including, but not limited to, patriarchy, racism and religious fundamentalism of all creeds. We embrace the full dignity of all human beings. 3) A confrontational attitude, since we do not think that lobbying can have a major impact in such biased and undemocratic organisations, in which transnational capital is the only real policy-maker; 4) A call to direct action and civil disobedience, support for social movements' struggles, advocating forms of resistance which maximize respect for life and oppressed peoples' rights, as well as the construction of local alternatives to global capitalism; 5) An organisational philosophy based on decentralisation and autonomy (http: //www.nadir.org/nadir/initiativ/agp/en/).

22   According to a scathing article widely circulate on the Internet: "The US based sub-cultural cult 'Crimethinc' (CWC) who mix anarchism with bohemian drop-out lifestyles and vague anti-civilisation sentiment would have you believe that capitalism is something from which you can merely remove yourself by quitting work, eating from bins and doing whatever 'feels good.'" The author of the rant, written without paragraph breaks, disagreed (http://www.illegalvoices.org/apoc_blog/apoc_blog/rethinking_crimethinc_2.html).

23   A theme lifted directly from Raoul Vaneigem's Situationist classic *The Revolution of Everyday Life*.

Four: You Can't Do Gender in a Riot
24   Although the Black Bloc was not well known in North America prior to Seattle, anarchists have used the tactic on this continent since the early nineties. Early actions included mobilizations against Operation Desert Storm in 1991 (cf. Ickibob 2003). The Black Bloc finds its origins in the German *Autonomen* tradition of the late seventies and eighties. This tradition, which grew out of the failures of the student mobilizations of the sixties, incorporated aspects of Marxist and anarchist politics and developed a number of cultural and political innovations that now inform many contemporary radical political campaigns (cf. Katsiafiacas 2006).

25 Defending the Black Bloc actions that took place during the April 16, 2000 mobilization against the IMF and World Bank in Washington DC, one activist proposed that "proportionately speaking, the black bloc may have been more diverse than the mobilization as a whole" (http://www.infoshop.org/octo/a16_a_kudos. html).

26 It's hard to dispute Dominick's assessment of the relative privilege needed in order to participate in anti-summit actions. However, to reduce the question of *resonance* to that of *attendance* grossly underestimates the pattern of diffusion that marks radical action. As Walter Benjamin pointed out in his "Critique of Violence," the acts of criminal outlaws resonate with people who would never commit similar acts (and might even find them repugnant) precisely because they stand as testament to the limits of a sovereign power to which they, too, are subordinated (1978: 281). In *The Wretched of the Earth*, Frantz Fanon described how the circulation of images and stories of struggle or atrocity prompts diverse regional mobilizations that gain political significance from their connection to a common referent (1963: 75–76). On a similar note, Ward Churchill has challenged the notion that people of color are more likely to participate in "inclusive" actions than politically effective ones. Describing the rituals of the predominantly white pacifist scene, Churchill is not surprised to find "that North America's ghetto, barrio, and reservation populations, along with the bulk of the white working class ... tend either to stand aside in bemused incomprehension of such politics or to react with outright hostility. Their apprehension of the need for revolutionary change and their conception of revolutionary dynamics are necessarily at radical odds with this notion of 'struggle'" (1998: 64).

27 This statement stands generally for liberals and left radicals in North America. The few notable exceptions take the form of ambiguous mobilizations like the Million Man March and groups like the Promise Keepers. However, even in these cases, the gender exclusive character of the phenomena is justified not on the basis of the general inadmissibility of women into politics but rather on what are perceived to be the specific historic responsibilities of the mobilized men.

28 It's a representational strategy that, as Richard Dyer has pointed out, underscores the constitutive contradictions of white ontology. In *White*, Dyer describes how the illumination of white subjects in painting, photography, and cinema discloses two interrelated but conflicting impulses. On the one hand, the illuminated subject is given a transcendental luster that dematerializes the everyday facts of embodiment, thus reiterating the pretense of omniscience underlying white epistemology. On the other hand, the implied transparency achieved by lighting of

this kind highlights the spectral anxieties underlying white ontology. The escape from the corporeal realm of everyday experience leaves the white knower anxious about the status of her presence (1997: 208–212). At its limits, this anxiety expresses itself as an association between whiteness and death.

29   Despite this omission, we are entitled to wonder how—if these organizations were as diffuse as he claims—Connolly could proclaim with any certainty that women did not also don white shirts. In *Transgender Warriors*, Leslie Feinberg writes the "White Boys" into the history of cross-dressing in an attempt to show the implicit militancy of gender transgression. In Feinberg's account, the "White Boys" drew upon the matrilineal interest in fairies as oppositional figures in order to oppose the Christian order with which they associated the landlords. The white shirts described by Connolly become women's dressing gowns (1996: 78–79). Although Feinberg's account is compelling, by focusing on the dynamics of cross-dressing rather than those of forging a collective "we," ze misses the possibility that the White Boys were a *cross-gender* alliance and not simply a cross-dressing one.

30   This acknowledgement becomes all the more significant when viewed through the lens of Jean-Paul Sartre's account of that event in *Critique of Dialectical Reason*. Sartre outlines how the act of storming the prison produced a fused group in which subjects began to realize themselves politically *through the Other* (2004: 351–363). Although he does not draw out his conclusions in relation to gender, it's easy to imagine how—when men and women begin to realize themselves through their counterpart—they simultaneously begin to forfeit the discrete character of their own gender identification.

31   Indeed, this transition seems to play itself out whenever civil disobedience advocates come to recognize the futility of their tactics in light of the intransigence of their opponents. One need only to consider the radical difference between Mario Savio's 1964 pronouncements during the Berkeley Free Speech Movement occupation of Sproul Hall and those spelled out by Bernardine Dohrn in the first Weatherman communiqué (1970: 509) to see how this is the case. Although both figures were important participants in the American student movement during the 1960s, their divergent political orientations show in no uncertain terms the difference a few years can make.

32   Consider, for instance, Fanon's account of the ontological transformation of the colonized in the moment of political violence as recounted in the opening section of *The Wretched of the Earth*: "the native discovers that his life, his breath, his beating heart are the same as those of the settler... All the new revolutionary

assurance of the native stems from it" (1963: 45).

33   The political distinction between the filiative (denoting the politics of being) and the affiliative (denoting the politics of belief) is neatly outlined in a recent work by Timothy Brennan (2006).

34   One recent example of this logic can be found in Richard Day's Book *Gramsci is Dead: Anarchist Currents in the Newest Social Movements*, where he describes how new movement tactics not only "refuse to deploy traditional tactics that seek to alter/replace existing modes of power/signification" but that "their own organizational structures are designed so as to avoid situations where one individual or group is placed 'above' others in hierarchical relationship" (2006: 45).

35   This observation accords with the basic premise of historical materialist analysis. As suggested by Marx in *The German Ideology*, social research must start with *people*—with what they do and what they've done—and work its way out. The premises of materialist analysis "are men, not in any fantastic isolation and fixity, but in their actual, empirically perceptible process of development under definite conditions" (1998: 43).

36   In a context where violence has often been unthinkable for women, the content of the "common" tactic is of secondary importance to the mobilization of violence itself. Nevertheless, it's evident that women's political use of violence will not be identical to conventional male uses of violence. The division can be understood using Benjamin's distinction between law-making and law-preserving violence (1978: 287). Since women, historically on the defensive, create a new dynamic in the everyday operations of sexism when they adopt violent means, their act can best be understood as a law making violence. However, in a social context where violence itself—rendered as a categorical abstraction—has been unthinkable, the ontological and political distinction between the two modes has sometimes been difficult to perceive.

37   It is in this context that we can understand how the simple phrase "do it" became an important slogan during the demonstrations against the G8 meeting in Gleneagles, Scotland during the summer of 2005 (http: //www.counterpunch. org/tina07122005.html).

Five: The Coming Catastrophe
38   For an account of this demonstration, see "WTO Protests Met With Police Pursuits, Mass Arrests" (http: //www.kersplebedeb.com/montreal/#WTO_PROTESTS).

39   In the Introduction to *Homo Sacer*, Giorgio Agamben highlights the connection between post-democratic spectacular societies such as those considered by Guy Debord and the colonial and totalitarian regimes that stand as their putative antitheses. "To become conscious of this aporia is not to belittle the accomplishments of democracy," he states. "It is, rather, to try to understand once and for all why democracy, at the very moment in which it seemed to have finally triumphed over its adversaries and reached its greatest heights, proved incapable of saving *zoë* [life as such], to whose happiness it had dedicated all its efforts, form unprecedented ruin" (1998: 10).

40   According to Ignatiev, "an 1847 census taker in Moyamensing-Southwark, describing the black population, wrote 'My heart is sick, my soul is horror-stricken at what my eyes behold… The greater part of these people live in with the Irish'" (129).

41   Ignatiev describes the situation as follows: "The city relied on volunteers to defend public order… In case of special need, special posses were sworn in, whose members carried neither guns nor wore badges. Behind the ad hoc volunteers stood the militia, a slightly more regular but also non-professional force" (132).

42   It's on this basis that we are often forced to endure conversations aimed at determining who is committing "the real violence." The common theme in these discussions is the desire to absolve demonstrators of any contact with violence and keep us innocent. Although framing the discussion in this way might prove to be strategically useful in the short term, the danger is that it makes it impossible to talk openly about violence's productive character and why activists have little choice but to consider it.

43   Many readers have dismissed Agamben's thesis as hyperbolic. Nevertheless, it's important to recognize that he has not been the only writer to advance arguments pointing to the intimate connection between the Holocaust and the modern world. In the closing passage of *Moments of Reprieve*, Holocaust survivor Primo Levi reminds us of how we—contemporary readers—are "so dazzled by power and money as to forget our essential fragility, forget that all of us are in the ghetto, that the ghetto is fenced in, that beyond the fence stand the lords of death, and not far away the train is waiting" (1995: 128). Adopting a more sociological tone, Zigmunt Bauman recounts how "the unspoken terror permeating our collective memory of the Holocaust … is the gnawing suspicion that the Holocaust could be more than an aberration… We suspect (even if we refuse to admit it) that the Holocaust could merely have uncovered another face of the same modern society whose other, more

familiar, face we so admire… What we perhaps fear most, is that each of the two faces can no more exist without the other than can the two sides of a coin" (2000: 7). To these accounts, we can add the whole of the critical theory tradition and, in particular, the work of Theodor Adorno whose writing was especially attentive to the threshold at which the rational turned into its other.

44   In the closing pages of *Days of War, Nights of Love*, CrimethInc include a poster featuring a hand grenade and a citation drawn from one of Durden's famous soliloquies.

45   For an excellent analysis of this dynamic, see Augusto Boal's *Theatre of the Oppressed* (1979).

46   CrimethInc even made it the subject of one of their early actions.

Coda: Representation's Limit

47   In his definitive historical account of the social movement as a discrete phenomenon, Charles Tilly emphasizes how the right to assembly, association, and speech that came into being under bourgeois rule provided the basis for social movement performances and routines, as well as a context for their displays of worthiness, unity, numbers, and commitment (2004: 64). All told, the social movement as we know it today is a child of the bourgeois revolution.

48   There are, of course, other possibilities. Constituted power could, for instance, act upon the claim maker before they are able to act upon either the public or upon constituted power. However, this schematic account is useful for highlighting the process as it arises in its pure form and in the first instance. It also helps to highlight the extent to which political processes follow predictable courses and how disruption involves elaborating strategies that work to reverse the flow of those processes.

49   As Ward Churchill and others have explained, the modern democratic state has made use of social movements as a kind of informal polling option. In this way, they have been able to repackage policies in order to make them more palatable without ever having to change overall policy direction (1998: 51–52).

50   The problem is analogous to the one arising from the relationship between cause and effect. Logically, the cause precedes the effect. However, in contemplation, effects are always noted first. The cause is thus produced through contemplation and *post festum*.

BIBLIOGRAPHY

ACME Collective (2001). "N30 Black Bloc Communiqué." *The Battle of Seattle: The New Challenge to Capitalist Globalization*. New York: Soft Skull Press

Agamben, Giorgio (1995). *Homo Sacer: Sovereign Power and Bare Life*. Stanford: Stanford University Press

Appadurai, Arjun (2000). "Grassroots Globalization and the Research Imagination." *Public Culture* 12 (1). Duke University Press

Arendt, Hannah (1970). *On Violence*. San Diego: Harcourt Brace & Company

Artaud, Antonin (1958). *The Theater and its Double*. New York: : Grove Press

Baldwin, James (1964). *The Fire Next Time*. New York: A Delta Book

Bannerji, Himani (2000). *Dark Side of the Nation: Essays on Multiculturalism, Nationalism and Gender*. Toronto: Canadian Scholars Press

Barnholden, Michael (2005). *Reading the Riot Act: A Brief History of Riots in Vancouver*. Vancouver: Anvil Press

Baudrillard, Jean (2002). *The Spirit of Terrorism*. London: Verso

Bauman, Zigmunt (2000). *Modernity and the Holocaust*. Ithaca, NY: Cornell University Press

Bell, Derrick (1992). *Faces at the Bottom of the Well: The Permanence of Racism*. New York: Basic Books

Benjamin, Walter (2003). *The Arcades Project*. Cambridge, MA: Harvard University Press

——. (1978). "Critique of Violence." *Reflections*. New York: Schocken Books

——. (1978). "Surrealism." *Reflections*. New York: Schocken Books

Beyer-Arnesen, Harald (2000). "Direct Action: Toward an Understanding of a Concept" *Anarcho-Syndicalist Review*, no. 29 (Summer 2000)

Black, Mary (2001). "Letter from Inside the Black Bloc." http: //squat.net/ tmc/msg01981.html. Retrieved January 1, 2007

Bloch, Ernst (2000). *The Spirit of Utopia*. Stanford, CA: Stanford University Press

Boal, Augusto (1985). *Theatre of the Oppressed*. New York: Theatre Communications Group

Brennan, Timothy (2006). *Wars of Position: The Cultural Politics of Left and Right*. New York: Columbia University Press

Butler, Judith (1990). *Gender Trouble: Feminism and the Subversion of Identity*. New York: Routledge

Carmichael, Stokely & Charles Hamilton (1967). *Black Power: The Politics of Liberation in America*. New York: Vintage Books

Camus, Albert (1988). *Resistance, Rebellion, and Death*. New York: Vintage Books

Churchill, Ward (1998). *Pacifism as Pathology: Reflections on the Role of Armed Struggle in North America*. Winnipeg: Arbeiter Ring

Clarke, John (2002). "Interrogation at the US Border." *Counterpunch*, February 25, 2002. http: //www.counterpunch.org/clarke1.html. Accessed January 1, 2003

Claustrophobia Collective (2001). *How Fast It All Blows Up: Some Lessons from the 2001 Cincinnati Riots*. St. Louis: One Thousand Emotions

Connolly, James (1987). *Labour in Irish History*. London: Bookmarks

CrimethInc (2001). *Days of War, Nights of Love: Crimethink for Beginners*. Atlanta: CrimethInc Free Press

———. (2003). *Evasion*. Atlanta: CrimethInc Free Press

CSIS (2000a). "2000 Public Report." August 12, 2001. http: //www.csis-crs.gc.ca/eng//publicrp/pub2000_e.html. Accessed December 10, 2001

CSIS (2000b). "Report #2000/08: Anti-Globalization—A Spreading Phenomenon." August 22, 2000. http: //www.csis-crs.gc.ca/eng/miscdocs/200008_e.html. Accessed December 1, 2001

Day, Richard (2005). *Gramsci is Dead: Anarchist Currents in the Newest Social Movements*. Toronto: Between the Lines

Debord, Guy (1990). *Comments on the Society of the Spectacle*. London: Verso

———. (1983). *Society of the Spectacle*. Detroit: Red and Black

de Toledo, Camille (2008). *Coming of Age at the End of History*. New York: Soft Skull Press

Dirks, Yutaka (2002). "Doing Things Differently This Time: Kananaskis G8 Meeting and Movement Building." http://www.infoshop.org/inews/article.php?story=02/02/10/3017765. Retrieved March 10, 2002

Dominick, Brian (2000). "Anarchy, Non/Violence, and the Seattle Actions." http://www.zmag.org/anarchynv.htm. Retrieved January 1, 2007

Duberman, Martin (2002). "Black Power And the American Radical Tradition." *Left Out—The Politics of Exclusion: Essays 1964–2002*. Cambridge: South End Press

Dworkin, Andrea (1987). *Intercourse*. New York: The Free Press

Dyer, Richard (1997). *White*. New York: Routledge

Elsaadi, Nabil (2001). "Who's the Thug?" *Now Magazine*, October 25, 2001, p. 19

Engels, Friedrich (1993). *The Condition of the Working Class in England*. Oxford and New York: Oxford University Press

Epstein, Barbara (2001). "Anarchism and the Anti-Globalization Movement." *Monthly Review* 53 (4), September 2001

Esmonde, Jackie (2002). "Bring the Struggle Home: Summit-Hopping or Organizing to Win." *New Socialist Magazine* 36

Fanon, Frantz (1967). *Black Skin, White Masks*. New York: Grove Press

——. (1963). *The Wretched of the Earth*. New York: Grove Press

Feinberg, Leslie (1996). *Transgender Warriors: Making History from Joan of Arc to Rupaul*. Boston: Beacon Press

Ferguson, Sarah (2000). "Demonstrate This." *The Village Voice*, August 15, 2000

Firestone, Shluamith (1970). *The Dialectic of Sex: The Case for Feminist Revolution*. New York: Farrar, Strauss and Giroux

Foran, John, ed. (2003). *The Future of Revolutions: Rethinking Radical Change in the Age of Globalization*. London and New York: Zed Books

Foster, Hal (2004). *Prosthetic Gods*. Cambridge, MA: The MIT Press

Foucault, Michel (1990). *The History of Sexuality: Volume 1*. New York: Vintage

——. (1988). *Madness and Civilization: A History of Insanity in the Age of Reason*. New York: Vintage Books

Frank, Joshua (2005). "Muzzled Activist in the Age of Terror." *Z Magazine*, April 2005. http: //www.ww.zcommunications.org/zmag/viewArticle/13765. Accessed January 1, 2006

Freeman, Carla (2001). "Is Local/Global as Feminine/Masculine? Rethinking the Gender of Globalization." *Signs* 26 (4) pp.1007–1037

Freire, Paulo (1993). *Pedagogy of the City*. New York: Continuum

——. (1996). *Pedagogy of the Oppressed*. New York: Continuum

Friedan, Betty (1963). *The Feminine Mystique*. New York: W.W. Norton & Company

Graham, Adam and Ariel Troster (1999). "The Link's Activist Toolbox: Everything You Need to Know to Be a Dissident in Montreal." *The Link* 20 (4), September 14, 1999, pp.14–15

Green Mountain Anarchist Collective (GMAC) (2000). *A Communique on Tactics and Organization: To the Black Bloc from Within the Black Bloc*. Multiple print runs (zine)

Guilloud, Stephanie (2003). "An Open Letter to Anti-Globalization Protestors, or: Why I Didn't Go to Miami." http: //colours.mahost.org/articles/guilloud.html. Retrieved March 7, 2007

Haraway, Donna (1991). *Simians, Cyborgs, and Women: The Reinvention of Nature*. New York: Routledge

Hoffman, Abbie (1969). *Woodstock Nation*. New York: Vintage Books

Holloway, John (2005). *Change the World Without Taking Power*. London: Pluto Press

Ickibob (2003). "On the Black Bloc." *A New World in Our Hearts: Eight Years of Writings from the Love and Rage Revolutionary Anarchist Federation*. Oakland: AK Press

Ignatiev, Noel (1995). *How the Irish Became White*. New York: Routledge

Infoshop.org (2001). "Black Bloc For Dummies." http: //infoshop.org/texts/ bb_tactics.html

Jackson, Laura (Riding) (1993). *The Word Woman and Other Related Writings*. New York: Persea Books

James, Joy (1997). *Transcending the Talented Tenth: Black Leaders and American Intellectuals*. New York: Routledge

Jameson, Fredric (1991). *Postmodernism or, The Cultural Logic of Late Capitalism*. Durham: Duke University Press

Jay, Martin (2003). *Refractions of Violence*. New York: Routledge

Joseph, Miranda (2002). *Against the Romance of Community*. Minneapolis: University of Minnesota Press

Katsiaficas, George (2006). *The Subversion of Politics: European Autonomous Social Movements and the Decolonization of Everyday Life*. Oakland: AK Press

Kanouse, Sarah (2005). "Cooing Over the Golden Phallus." *The Journal of Aesthetics and Protest* 1 (4). Los Angeles

Kaye/Kantrowitz, Melanie (1992). *The Issue is Power: Essays on Women, Jews, Violence and Resistance*. San Francisco: Aunt Lutte Press

Kingsnorth, Paul (2003). *One No, Many Yeses: A Journey to the Heart of the Global Resistance Movement*. London: The Free Press

Klein, Naomi (2000). "Does Protest Need a Vision?" http://www.newstatesman.com/200007030017. Retrieved February 26, 2007

Levi, Primo (1995). *Moments of Reprieve: A Memoir of Auschwitz*. New York: Penguin Books

Lloyd, Trevor (1971). *Suffragettes International: The World-wide Campaign for Women's Rights*. Great Britain: Library of the 20th Century

Lorde, Audre (1984). *Sister Outsider*. Freedom, CA: The Crossing Press

MacKinnon, JB. (2000). "The Usual Suspects." *This Magazine*, July/August 2000

Martinez, Elizabeth (2000). "Where Was the Color in Seattle?" *Colorlines*, Spring 2000

Marx, Karl (1977). *Capital, Volume 1*. Moscow: Progress Publishers

——. (1964). *The Economic and Philosophic Manuscripts of 1844*. New York: International Publishers

——. (1969). "The Eighteenth Brumaire of Louis Bonaparte." *Karl Marx and Friedrich Engels: Selected Works, Volume 1*. Moscow: Progress Publishers

Marx, Karl and Friedrich Engels (1998). *The German Ideology*. Amherst, NY: Prometheus Books

McNally, David (2002). *Another World Is Possible: Globalization and Anti-Capitalism*. Winnipeg: Arbeiter Ring Publishing

Mohanram, Radhika (1999). *Black Body: Women, Colonialism, and Space*. Minneapolis: University of Minnesota Press

Mohanty, Chandra Talpade (1995). "Feminist Encounters: Locating the Politics of Experience." *Social Postmodernism: Beyond Identity Politics*. Cambridge and New York: Cambridge University Press

Momboisse, Raymond (1967). *Riots, Revolts and Insurrections*. Springfield: Charles C. Thomas Publisher

Monagham, Jeff and Kevin Walby (2008). "The Green Scare Is Everywhere: The Importance of Cross-Movement Solidarity." *Upping the Anti: A Journal of Theory and Action*, No. 6. Toronto

Munroe, Jim (1998). "Playing Revolution." *This Magazine*, November. Toronto

Neumann, Rachel (2001). "A Place for Rage." *The Battle of Seattle: The New Challenge to Capitalist Globalization*. New York: Soft Skull Press

Nye, Andrea (1990). *Words of Power: A Feminist Reading of the History of Logic*. New York: Routledge

Ollman, Bertell (1971). *Alienation: Marx's Conception of Man in Capitalist Society*. New York: Cambridge University Press

Orwell, George (2001). *The Road to Wigan Pier*. London: Penguin Books

Palahniuk, Chuck (1996). *Fight Club*. New York: Henry Holt and Company

Phillips, Melanie (2003). *The Ascent of Women: A History of the Suffragette Movement and the Ideas Behind It*. London: Abacus

Razack, Sherene H., ed. (2002). *Race, Space, and the Law: Unmapping a White Settler Society*. Toronto: Between the Lines

Rebick, Judy (2002). "Lip Service: The Anti-Globalization Movement on Gender Politics." *Herizons*. http://www.accessmylibrary.com/coms2/summary_0286–2167758_ITM. Retrieved January 1, 2007

Rose, Nikolas (1999). *Powers of Freedom: Reframing Political Thought*. Cambridge and New York: Cambridge University Press

Rowbotham, Sheila (1974). *Women, Resistance & Revolution: A History of Women and Revolution in the Modern World*. New York: Vintage

Rubin, Jerry (1970). *Do It! Scenarios of the Revolution.* New York: Simon and Schuster

Said, Edward (1979). *Orientalism.* New York: Vintage Books

Sanbonmatsu, John (2004). *The Postmodern Prince: Critical Theory, Left Strategy, and the Making of a New Political Subject.* New York: Monthly Review Press

Sartre, Jean-Paul (2004). *Critique of Dialectical Reason: Volume One.* London: Verso

——. (1971). *Sketch for a Theory of the Emotions.* London: Methuen and & Co Ltd

Schmid, Alex P. and Jenny de Graaf (1982). *Violence as Communication: Insurgent Terrorism and the Western News Media.* London: SAGE Publications

Sekyi-Oyu, Ato (1996). *Fanon's Dialectic of Experience.* Cambridge, MA: Harvard University Press

Smith, Dorothy (1990). *The Conceptual Practices of Power: A Feminist Sociology of Knowledge.* Toronto: University of Toronto Press

Smith, George (1990). "Political Activist as Ethnographer." *Social Problems* 37 (4), November 1990

Sorel, Georges (2004). *Reflections on Violence.* Mineola, NY: Dover

Spivak, Gayatri Chakravorty (1988). "Can the Subaltern Speak?" *Marxism and the Interpretation of Culture* (Cary Nelson and Lawrence Grossberg, eds.). Urbana: University of Illinois Press

Starr, Amory (2005). *Global Revolt: A Guide to the Movements Against Globalization.* New York: Zed Books

Thoreau, Henry David (1960). *Civil Disobedience.* Boston: The Riverside Press

Tilly, Charles (2004). *Social Movements, 1768–2004*. Boulder, CO: Paradigm Publishers

Tobocman, Seth (1999). *War in the Neighborhood: A Graphic Novel*. New York: Autonomedia

Touraine, Alain (1981). *The Voice and the Eye*. Cambridge: Cambridge University Press

Trotsky, Leon (1973). *Their Morals and Ours: Marxist vs. Liberal Views on Morality*. New York: Pathfinder Press.

Vaneigem, Raoul (1967, 2003). *The Revolution of Everyday Life*. London: Rebel Press

Wainwright, Hillary (November 20, 2003). "The Importance of the Local." *Znet*. http://zmag.org/content/print_article.cfm?itemID=4534&sectionID=41

Wallace, Michele (1990). *Black Macho and the Myth of the Superwoman*. New York: Verso

Weatherman Underground (1970). "Communique #1 From the Weatherman Underground." *Weatherman* (Harold Jacobs, ed.). Ramparts Press, Inc.

Zizek, Slavoj (1992, 2008). *Enjoy Your Symptom!* New York: Routledge

——. (2002). *Welcome to the Desert of the Real*. London: Verso

INDEX

Support AK Press!

AK Press is one of the world's largest and most productive  anarchist publishing houses. We're entirely worker-run and democratically managed. We operate without a corporate structure—no boss, no managers, no bullshit. We publish close to twenty books every year, and distribute thousands of other titles published by other like-minded independent presses from around the globe.

The Friends of AK program is a way that you can directly contribute to the continued existence of AK Press, and ensure that we're able to keep publishing great books just like this one! Friends pay a minimum of $25 per month, for a minimum three month period, into our publishing account. In return, Friends automatically receive (for the duration of their membership), as they appear, one free copy of every new AK Press title. They're also entitled to a 20% discount on everything featured in the AK Press Distribution catalog and on the website, on any and every order. You or your organization can even sponsor an entire book if you should so choose!

There's great stuff in the works—so sign up now to become a Friend of AK Press, and let the presses roll!

Won't you be our friend? Email friendsofak@akpress.org for more info, or visit the Friends of AK Press website:
http://www.akpress.org/programs/friendsofak